Single Seed

SONG OF SONGS 2 : 7

SINGLE SEED

BY JEMMA VALERIE HARLEY DREYER

REACH PUBLISHERS

Published by Jemma Dreyer using Reach Publishers' services,
P O Box 1384, Wandsbeck, South Africa, 3631

Edited by Ian Milne for Reach Publishers
Cover designed by Reach Publishers
Website: www.reachpublishers.org
E-mail: reach@reachpublishers.org

Jemma Dreyer

jemma.dreyer@gmail.com

Note – If I have included any extracts for the use of which I should have obtained permission but have failed so to do, I would ask the Author or Publisher concerned to accept my sincere apologies – J.V.H.D

INTRODUCTION

Song of Songs 2:7 (NIV)

Daughters of Jerusalem, I charge you by the gazelles and by the does of the field: Do not arouse love until it so desires.

More often than not, a single season can bring emotions that may consume your youth. It disrupts the value of clarity. It would be difficult to fall deep or even dig deep and not have a way or plan out. I believe that a single season is the fruitful aspect one needs in life. Among other important characteristics, this season builds character and allows you to identify who you are. A seed is planted in the womb of a woman to carry a child. It is in this image that we experience God through us, "creation". When you understand your natural order, it is easier to recognise the way in which God created life to be. The purpose of this book is to unpack traumas in your life, to deal with hidden and unjust comparisons, to figure out what you want out of life and for you to utilise this season in its greatest capacity. God is infinite and mysterious; however, God does not shun or withhold truth, discipline and success.

It is important to remember that seasons don't last forever, they are varied, and getting too comfortable may result in speedy transformation and change. Refining is a slow time consuming process and having rapid change can mutilate the final product. In this single season don't become faint. We all grow up in what we see as normal. As we mature mentally and spiritually, we begin to recognise times and wounds that we would not want to take into our own family. It is important not to go into relationships and marriage with baggage, and it is also fundamental to fully understand THE CONCEPT OF LOVE through God's lens. Asking questions like Am I really in love? Am I Beautiful? Can I become who and what God has promised? Is it healthy/Godly to have this amount of overwhelming depression and anxiety? It is vital to have these questions answered by God.

The single season is not just a waiting season; it's one of planting, uprooting, cultivating and nurturing.

I pray God breathes into your heart and mind as you journey through a door that God has laid out for you. Divine opportunity and intervention calls for correction, guidance and renewed love.

Intentional Singleness

INTENTIONAL   *Done on purpose, deliberate.*

SINGLENESS   *The quality or state of being single (unmarried).*

Song of Songs 2:7

Daughters of Jerusalem, I charge you by the gazelles and by the does of the field: Do not arouse love until it so desires.

Intentional singleness is a concept or idea known to many Christians, but not truly understood. Intentional singleness is a season birthed out of the will of God, allowing many to find identity, purpose, passion, compassion, drive and so much more; the singleness season is vast in its ways and so effective if done with intentionality and full pursuit of Jesus Christ.

To be intentional is to be deliberate. Don't just allow your single season to pass without knowledge of what God wanted to teach you or what experiences you needed to learn from over this time. Often the trials and experiences in our single season foreshadow what's to come. How we handle our singleness and how we take care of ourselves, is what we will one day impart to our spouse and children.

An intentional season of singleness is one of utmost importance and wisdom. The knowledge of God is crucial to a seeking heart and wondering mind, it transforms one mindset to another, and it shifts the way we not only see things, but also how we do things.

Regardless of where you find yourself in this season, as much as we pursue God, He opens up and allows us to see more of who He is and His character. A deep-rooted relationship with God is a solid foundation, and when coming out of the singles season it becomes the centre and solid foundation for a marriage to stand on.

In your intentionality, allow yourself to be teachable and loved by God, hold steadfast to the faith that carries all from start to finish. Have an adaptable nature that allows the Holy Spirit to be so tangible, to create an atmosphere and aroma so pure that any distraction or weapon formed will bow at the purity and immovable hope in Christ Jesus. Trust that this season brings seeds and fruit like no other and be made new in a season Paul calls a GIFT (1 Cor 7:7-8).

Allow Him to Sweep You Off Your Feet Before Anyone Else Does

SWEEP   *To move swiftly and smoothly.*

FEET   *Defined as the part of the body that touches the ground.*

Psalm 139

O Lord, you have searched me and you know me.

You know when I sit and when I rise you perceive my thoughts from afar.

You discern my going out and my lying down.

You are familiar with all my ways.

Before a word is on my tongue, you know it completely, O Lord,

You hem me in behind and before, you have laid your hand upon me.

Such knowledge is too wonderful for me, too lofty for me to attain.

Where can I go from your spirit?

Where can I flee from your presence?

If I go up to the heavens, you are there; if I make my bed in the depths, you are there. If I rise on the wings of the dawn, if I settle on the far side of the sea, even there your hand will guide me, your right hand will hold me fast.

If I say, "Surely the darkness will hide me and the light become night around me", even the darkness will not be dark to you, the night will shine like the day, for darkness is as light to you.

For you created my inmost being; you knit me together in my mother's womb.

I praise you because I am fearfully and wonderfully made; your works are wonderful, I know that full well.

My frame was not hidden from you when I was made in the secret place.

When I was woven together in the depths of the earth,

Your eyes saw my unformed body.

All the days ordained for me

Were written in your book

Before one of them came to be.

How precious to me are your thoughts, O God!

How vast is the sum of them!

Were I to count them, they would outnumber the grains of sand. When I awake, I am still with you.

If only you would slay the wicked, O' God!

Away from me, you bloodthirsty men!

They speak of you with evil intent, your adversaries misuse your name.

Do I not hate those who hate you O Lord and abhor those who rise up against you?

I have nothing but hatred for them,

I count them my enemies.

Search me, O God, and know my heart, test me and know my anxious thoughts.

See if there is any offensive way in me, and lead me in the way everlasting.

According to Google, the word God is defined as: "God, in monotheistic thought, is conceived of as the supreme being, creator, deity and principal object of faith. God is usually conceived as being omnipotent (all-powerful), omniscient (all knowing), omnipresent (all present) and omnibenevolent (all good), as well as having an eternal and necessary existence".

I believe this to be true. Add **is** to "God is" and see how, under any philosophy, the full character of God cannot be attained nor fully understood. God is so diverse and multifaceted that our minds would shatter at the comprehensive and overflowing uprightness of God, His righteousness and integrity. For example, in Genesis

1:27 it speaks of how God created mankind in His own image. Our world is so rich in race, culture and heritage, yet the Bible says we are created in His image.

Racism, discrimination and bias are, and have been, an ongoing issue for many people of colour, women, and individuals with disability, to name but a few; I think this type of diversity is an illustration of how diverse our heavenly Father is and just how relatable and flexible (unbreakable) He is. We as human individuals have decided what race is superior, whether women are less than men, or that a disability is proof that something went wrong , but the truth is God doesn't make mistakes and calling His creation a mistake, calls His very nature a mistake, meaning error, fault, inaccurate, or imperfect. Now if our human minds can't even understand one aspect of God's character, which in this case is diversity, how even more challenging is it for God to show all of Himself to a people who, with no education, insight or evidence of their conclusion, question, ridicule and persecute the ideology of God.

This is why, when we seek God, He also seeks us and guides us towards full understanding, comprehension, tolerance and awareness, as well as giving us a sympathetic edge for empathy and compassion to be open to transformation and a renewing of a sort. Back to the added **IS:** according to Google

The word "is" is considered as a verb, because it expresses existence or a state of being.

Now, when you allow God to sweep you off your feet, it means allowing Him to search and cleanse your inner being, your existence. Purifying the content of mind, body, soul and spirit.

In return He gives us the pleasure and honour of knowing Him on a deeper, more intimate level. Giving the human heart access into the very heart of God.

Allow God's permanent filling of affirmations, love, peace, kindness, joy and beauty to overwhelm you. Break away from distraught thinking, shut down lies, recognise them for what they are: deceitful.

Connect and communicate with your Father. Unveil the deep and heavy unknown and unseen mysteries of your life. And permit God's profound provision, freedom and timing to overtake your will.

ONLY YOU

O' Wonderful wind of the Holy Sprit

Guide me continually

Refresh my crater, it runs empty without you.

Boost my heart with love to move on.

Shine your face on my face, hands and heart so that I may know,

And so that they may see

It's only You.

PSALM 90:12 So teach us to number our days, that we may apply our hearts unto wisdom.

The Beauty of a Wife

Beauty, by definition, is the quality or aggregate of qualities in a person or thing that gives pleasure to the senses or pleasurably exalts the mind or spirit.

For further understanding/reference, read **Proverbs 31:10-31.**

Epilogue: The Wife of Noble Character

Beauty is the pinnacle of what people look for in most things. Beauty is attractive to the eye, but it can also be an attraction to the heart. Many long for beauty in order, the materialistic, and the physical appearance, and in internal worth. I, however, think beauty is when something is in its purest form, beauty creates a sense of wonder and mystery, and it is intriguing. Although we all have different perceptions of beauty, I came across a most beautiful quote: saying "Another woman's beauty is not the absence of your own" (Unknown).

This quote broke down every obscure, hidden idea I had about me, and I was no longer daunted by a sense of insecurity when I was amongst many other women.

Proverbs 31 outlines these facts about women:

- She sets about her work vigorously; her arms are strong for her tasks: STRONG
- She opens her arms to the poor and extends her hands to the needy: KIND/GENEROUS
- When it snows, she has no fear for her household: FEARLESS
- She is clothed with strength and dignity: she can laugh at the days to come: JOYFUL
- She speaks with wisdom, and faithful instruction is on her tongue: FAITH & WISDOM
- Many women do noble things, but you surpass them all: ONE OF A KIND

This is true beauty. The characteristics and content of your soul. Yes, beauty can be enhanced by a dress, hair, makeup and maybe even a pair of stunning shoes. But the confident and worthy, masterpiece that fits her righteous and holy personality, spirit and intelligent mind, are worth far more than rubies.

Rubies symbolise nobility, purity and passion. Things and qualities that can't be bought nor sold.

The aim is not to strive to be beautiful. Beauty is already within you. Engraved in your DNA. The aim is to see this type of flawless, authentic, sterling, uncontaminated beauty within you. Stop striving and simply accept who you are in God!

Time and Timing

The following verse is recommended to readers for further understanding/reference:

Ecclesiastes 3:1-8 (A time for everything)

Time: the indefinite continued progress of existence and sequence of events in the past, present and future, regarded as a whole, meets perfection (God), resulting in a flawless state where everything is exactly right; In the fullness of time.

John 11:17

"On his arrival, Jesus found that Lazarus had already been in the tomb for four days."

Our imperfect nature and sinful world is subject to the constraints of time. But when perfection enters, the limitation and restriction of time falls at the feet of Jesus.

Time not only sings a different song or melody, but it is also on a different wavelength compared to most things in life. Time is precious and is to be treasured. Time is speed, depth and definition. The Lord's timing is perfect. The stars, galaxies, waters, waves and even the breath a human inhales and exhales is perfectly timed.

Time is also undefined. It stops only when God says so, which is known to no one but God.

Time = Detail (nothing is wasted) Jeremiah 29:11

To concentrate on time is foolish. But to focus on the One who created it and spoke it into existence is wisdom. Yes, you are in a waiting season for your future spouse, but this is a special, set apart time. Fix your concentration on the truth that he who finds a wife (in time) finds a good thing. Don't try to grab just any opportunity but wait for your pre-destined time, and live eagerly anticipating the arrival of new seeds for your Individual needs and spirituality.

Habakkuk 2:2-3

Then the Lord replied: "Write down the revelation and make it plain on tablets so that a herald may run with it. For the revelation awaits an appointed time, it speaks of the end and will not prove false. Though it linger, wait for it, it will certainly come and will not delay."

It will not delay. For God's timing is perfect and cannot be measured or explained. It's in the detail.

Don't track time, don't analyse detail, don't try to outwit destiny, don't stalk purpose, don't chase dreams; follow them. Don't go after goals; run after them. God has carefully scheduled and arranged a plan for our lives that fits His time (time doesn't exist to God; He is aware of it and created it but works outside of it). His plan abandons organised human sociological imagination and practices, and sets an example of divine, incomparable, idyllic, quintessential, consummate, faultless and flawless power through which heaven cheers us on when we fulfil the pre-destined plan and will of God for our lives.

You are where you are supposed to be in time. At this moment, who you know, who you love, the knowledge you have, your position and social status is in perfect alignment with God's will.

You are His and you are in His master plan, but only time will tell when He reveals Himself to you and the manner in which He will do that.

Psalm 31:15

My times are in your hands; deliver me from the hands of my enemies, from those who pursue me.

El tiempo de Dios es perfecto: (God's time is perfect)

"A clock, the symbol or image – relating to God's image – of time, is circular, which symbolises a covenant, which is something whole and perfect".

Too Familiar
with Heartbreak

Heartbreak and loss to me has felt like a never-ending season. Grief is no catalyst for change, but a catalyst for defeat. I relied on God yet felt the baggage of loss; as if I lost the battles while the enemy won the wars. Nobody knew my shattered heart that was slowly turning cold, hard and so far, not only from reality but purpose. But brokenness is not the end. I felt my race was finished as if life just wasn't for me. I felt I didn't deserve to breathe fresh air freely, after all, many people have had a harder or more challenging life than mine. I felt my loss and grief were not painful enough, and that what I was feeling was in my imagination and I should just get over myself.

Yet through my pain and mundane daily routine carrying such heavy burdens, God's mandate never left. Even though I carried paid-for baggage that could not be stolen because Jesus bought it from us all. He had the grace to allow me to gather myself and to re-find who I am in Him a second time around. The journey of life doesn't start when you are born, it starts when you say "yes" to Jesus. True, trials and tribulations may be experienced on a walk with Jesus. Christians may be broken and confused, but that is God working through afflictions and making people whole by filling those gaps with Himself.

Don't underestimate the pain of life you have gone through or your experiences. Stand confident in Christ with the love and knowledge to know He will use all your experiences, good and bad, to His glory. For He is so infinitely vast and all powerful that our minds can't fathom or bear His image. No heart can fathom the thoughts and plans God has for us. "No eye has seen, nor ear has heard, nor heart imagined the plans I have for those who love me" (1 Corinthians 2:9) He says.

****

Come back but come back running. Run out of desperation. Run to the Father and wait. Wait for Him to respond. Don't think you can get through it on your own. My stubborn heart and mind can testify to this mistake first hand. Just as the bible says, "I can do all things through Christ who strengthens me" (Philippians 4:13). I am more than aware of the fact that I cannot do anything without my Father, Helper, Protector, and Friend beside me.

So lay down your burdens, for His burden is light and His yoke is easy. Come back to Jesus as your broken, whole philosophised self(whole fundamental nature of oneself). And sit and wait for the Father as you would wait for someone you can't live without to come out of that coma, that water, that fire, that depression or even as simple as that building. Pour yourself out as a sacrifice of love. Our Father operates through love. It's the foundation of life.

Love those who threaten your very existence. Revenge and vengeance is not our mandate or task to fulfil, because we simply cannot deliver out of a full loving nature. But God, Creator of love, will pursue those who curse Him and give them the same grace He has given us.

Be patient with those you lead and even more with those you follow; for they too are learning. Brokenness and heartbreak do not respect any man, and are ruthless and relentless at their mission.

Find healing and peace in Jesus and live free from every sin and condemnation the enemy brought to earth, for we are just passing through. This is not our home but our influence is greater than those whose names are on billboards. For we have the opportunity for greater community and fellowship. To know people not only by name or number but by their deep and affectionate love for Jesus and others. To walk a rough, painful and sometimes uncomfortably narrow path with them so that one day our family will be made whole in heaven as they will one day be on earth.

Don't let your pain and heartbreak distract you from your great calling. Saving souls, casting out demons, breaking chains and taking back land and people stolen from us.

Daniel 12:2-3

Multitudes who sleep in the dust of the earth will awake, some to everlasting life, others to shame and everlasting contempt. Those, who are wise will shine like the brightness of the heavens, and those who lead many to righteousness, like, the stars forever and ever.

This is the great commission:

Matthew 28:16-20 (New International Version)

****

The Great Commission

16 Then the eleven disciples went to Galilee, to the mountain where Jesus had told them to go. 17 When they saw him, they worshiped him; but some doubted. 18 Then Jesus came to them and said: "All authority in heaven and on earth has been given to me. 19 Therefore go and make disciples of all nations, baptizing them in

the name of the Father and of the Son and of the Holy Spirit, 20 and teaching them to obey everything I have commanded you. And surely I am with you always, to the very end of the age."

FOR YOU!

Dear anxious heart, be not troubled by the wind nor the sun, fade the noise, quiet the screams.

Break the bondage, filter the iniquity, plunge the heartbreak, defeat tiredness and tenderness.

Cry out, lament, and fall to your knees. For your prayers fall not on deaf ears, loneliness is but a season and a season fit for you.

I am with you, carrying your heart, My precious one, fight, fight for you, allow, allow yourself to be loved by Me, break, break the manner of contentment. I'm in the quiet silence, I'm in the chaos, I'm in the brokenness, I'm in the field of happiness, I'm on the mountain of joy. I'm in the melt down; I'm in the feelings and lack of them. I am everywhere and I will always be here, now run and don't turn back for your call is for you alone.

Many are called and a few are chosen but for you who accept My roar. You I have set apart for My glory, so cry, let it out, for what comes after is far greater than all the pain, affliction and trauma this world could ever throw at you.

It's okay to feel, I am not a God that would leave you. I am here for the water break you take; I am here for the breath of fresh air you come up for. I am here.

I am absolutely in awe and in love with who you are.

Pain in Capacity

Capacity:

- The maximum amount that something can contain.

- The amount that something can produce.

****

If your pain is measured in a jar, how much would it measure, would it overflow, would the jar be half full, would the jar break? How do you measure the pain you have endured?

Luke 12:48

From everyone who has been given much, much will be demanded.

Meaning that a great call requires great endurance. An increase in capacity can come in many ways and may be experienced through a variety of means, none of which can grow and stretch you like pain does. Pain produces fruits like no other, not just compassion and empathy, but it allows you to dive deeper into your spirit and to have an inside look into your identity and the way you subconsciously operate. Pain is financially exclusive and inclusive, meaning rich or poor, pain will educate. I believe the pain we endure in our lives is not punishment, nor is it just for us to learn but it is also for the benefit of our brothers and sisters. For us to lead by example, completing this race called life, we are not only called to be vessels, but also strong pillars which people and fellow believers can look up to and draw courage and strength from. Don't despise your pain and don't look down on those who break when pain starts manifesting but stand firm in the righteousness Jesus paid for. A strong or great capacity for pain is a force. Not just the cliché force to be reckoned with but a force unbound and untamed, a force unshakeable. You were made for this, to endure, to lead, to build and to conquer. Pain is scattered over the earth to build a better, stronger kingdom. So that nations are not born out of pride or an egotistical nature, but out of weakness. When I am weak, He is strong. Jesus used pain to pay the price on the cross and I believe pain is the paving we are to follow, and when we have endured great pain, heartbreak, sadness and grief, we are made new and can continue to pursue Jesus and step into our calling.

****

Don't strive for pain, but don't turn away when it comes knocking. Be gracious to yourself and show yourself the same mercy you show others. Forgive those who cause pain so that the receiving and letting go can be painless. Remain upright in your strength, don't break or take offense at words spoken against you. For we are image bearers, and we are made in God's likeness, and when they slander you for your obedience, they slander themselves in their own disobedience against God. Fear not and endure always, for He is the Good Shepherd that guides us to green pastures and quiet waters. Allow your peace to emerge at the blink of an eye for we are not from this world but just passing through.

On the Perspective of Not Being Able to Enter

Tell Him I am faint with distress

Panic overwhelms me

Manic frightens me.

The beast of my fear has been wakened

The minor chaos now outspoken

Tell Him I can't access the portal

The page unavailable

Comfort replaced by anguish

Prepared focus can now not be accomplished.

Where are my connections, the ones that lack infections?

Does one identify this philosophy or count on it as prophecy?

My heart beckons the rage

Please unleash this cage

Tell Him I am faint with distress

This soul can't find rest.

Hosea 10:12 (NIV)

Sow for yourselves righteousness, reap the fruit of unfailing love, and break up your unploughed ground, for it is time to seek the Lord, until He comes and showers His righteousness on you.

Yours for keeps

Counter thy fire
Break thy works
Fight thy temptation
Empty thy ways.

Foul and few are the cities
But you are a nation, a capital.
From wonders to the seas
Thy hand creates depth in me.

Opportunity lifts my cry
Justice for my sake
A safe haven for my promises
The doubts are like traps.

But pass me Thy will
For Thy hand scatters not my purpose.
I find passion in Thy palace,
Pillars in Thy provision,

And fields of well-nurtured victory.

I am Yours for keeps and You are my unfailing love.

****

Psalm 142 (NIV)

I cry aloud to the Lord; I lift up my voice to the lord for mercy. I pour out my complaint before Him; before Him I tell my trouble.

When my spirit grows faint within me, it is You who watch over my way. In the path where I walk people have hidden a snare for me. Look and see, there is no one at my right hand; no one is concerned for me. I have no refuge; no one cares for my life.

I cry to You, Lord, I say, "You are my refuge, my portion in the land of the living."

Listen to my cry, for I am in desperate need, rescue me from those who purse me, for they are too strong for me. Set me free from my prison, that I may praise Your name. Then the righteous will gather about me because of Your goodness to me.

Foreign

I hide my face,

I feel foreign in my own region.

Deadly are the swords that fall from their mouths

Deceitful are the hands that reach out to protect.

Do mortals lack capacity? Do they find freedom in captivity?

Curses hold no streets in heaven.

We are in heavenly places; they are not forbidden.

Music to my soul will help teach our way home. Stay then not hidden.

Rescue me, I hide my purpose

I feel foreign in my own religion.

I lack the grit to plough

My work is not done.

If I forever feel foreign

May the God of ages find a region to make my own, to call my home.

The following verse is recommended to readers for further understanding/reference: **Proverbs 4 (Get Wisdom at Any Cost)**

Face Value

Countless times it has gone too far,

I rise above, I raise the bar.

Fear, few and far in-between

Clear my heart so that I may glean.

The pressure to produce in seasons barren

The call upon cost to fathom

Future worlds I lead now,

Under the pressure I count on Thee.

The roots dive deep

The success under the soil and pinning the righteous.

Our lives show the heavenly fruit of a generous God

Down here on earth at face value.

Matthew 5:14-16

You are the light of the world. A town built on a hill cannot be hidden. Neither do people light a lamp and put it under a bowl. Instead they put it on its stand, and

it gives light to everyone in the house. In the same way let your light shine before others, that they may see your good deeds and glorify your Father in heaven.

A GOOD WIFE

Isaiah 40:3-5

A voice of one calling:
"In the wilderness prepare
    the way for the Lord[a];
make straight in the desert
    a highway for our God. [b]
4 Every valley shall be raised up,
    every mountain and hill made low;
the rough ground shall become level,
    the rugged places a plain.
5 And the glory of the Lord will be revealed,
    and all people will see it together.
For the mouth of the Lord has spoken."

Isaiah 40:11-15

He tends his flock like a shepherd:
    He gathers the lambs in his arms

and carries them close to his heart;

    he gently leads those that have young.

Who has measured the waters in the hollow of his hand,

    or with the breadth of his hand marked off the heavens?

Who has held the dust of the earth in a basket,

    or weighed the mountains on the scales

    and the hills in a balance?

Who can fathom the Spirit of the Lord,

    or instruct the Lord as his counselor?

Whom did the Lord consult to enlighten him,

    and who taught him the right way?

Who was it that taught him knowledge,

    or showed him the path of understanding?

Surely the nations are like a drop in a bucket;

    they are regarded as dust on the scales;

    he weighs the islands as though they were fine dust.

****

To my husband.

May the words I utter never fade away like the world.

May the peace of my heart reflect the presence of God in all seasons,

May my I LOVE YOU find a central stature that shall guide your compass,

May my love for you remain like God's grace, unfailing and adaptable.

May my intentions be as true as His word.

May my heart be as teachable as the disciples, as pure and divine as the call of David.

May I be your refreshing bride, the bride that reflects the church, pleasing in the eyes of the Lord and with whom He is well pleased.

I pray I'd be a good bride, in every way!

If We Don't Limit Our Imagination, Why Limit Your Reality

1 Timothy 1:5

The goal of this command is love, which comes from a pure heart and a good conscience and a sincere faith.

In many aspects of life one can combat one's reality and can make sense of most things. Our imagination is one place where we feel a great amount of freedom and an unlimited capacity. To dream a dream is one thing, but for it to come to pass is a gift we could never repay.

We often feel that we can't escape our reality, meaning we feel that our current day to day stride won't change. I have often dreamt, and believed wholeheartedly, that if God gave me this God dream, and He keeps to His promises, it will happen.

On another day I feel that a problem which is not my fault or that I didn't cause, is ultimately my responsibility, disregarding absolutely everything God had spoken over me.

I think in life we need balance, but we also need to choose a side. If confidence in Christ is where you found security when you said yes to Jesus, how then could you now go back on your own beliefs, questioning your own identity and moral compass?

One of the biggest things I've learnt in my short, yet full life, is that a God-given dream is a hope to some, a type of intimacy to many and a different perspective to all.

In Exodus 32:14 (KJV) it speaks of: "And the Lord repented of the evil which he thought to do unto his people" and at first glimpse of this verse, one could immediately question how it could be possible that an insanely great God should repent.

In fact, repentance to a mere mortal is a change of mindset and a second chance. Repentance to God is a change of method, not for a second chance, but simply because we didn't submit fully or grow in what He had first said; this can be traced back all the way to Genesis, and I suspect that it will go into the end of time. When we dream, we should go in with the mindset spoken of in 1 Timothy 1:5 (NIV): "The goal of this command is love, which comes from a pure heart and a good conscience and a sincere faith." When we approach our dreams and goals with love, a pure heart, clear conscience and sincere faith, that is the ultimate point of preparation. Dreaming for self-gain, money, or to feel like someone special, has a negative impact on your reality.

So back to: if we don't limit our imagination, why limit your reality? My simple outline is that if we limit our reality we limit God. God can work out and birth many things in your imagination, but it is in reality where faith in action is awakened , wild, and so bright. Reality is real life, and when we start processing and operating the way God intended, then we can recognise when provision is placed into our imagination, and understand that it doesn't stay there, that over time it becomes reality, and is fulfilled. God gives us dreams, He places things in our heart and spirit. The idea is not that you chase those dreams, it's that you place your full trust in Jesus and allow the outworking of the promise to meet God's will and match it with your reality.

Sitting Together

Let's sit in the sun together

And hope it lasts forever

Let's burn in this weather

And we can invite whoever.

But if it's just you and me

Don't rope to be free

Stretch your arm around me,

And

Let comfort be

The love you and I both see.

Feelings

1 Corinthians 13:13 (NIV)

"And now these three remain: faith, hope and love. But the greatest of these is love". I often felt unworthy, unloved, broken, and gone (as if I had disappeared into thin air). A place where all my passions die, my pain is hidden, and the small simple things disguise it as most beautiful.

Even in those moments love lingers and vibrates the heaviness of life until it is broken up. Love is the root of all good. Love positions us into the lens of God. No matter where we are, how far we have run, we are always in his view.

I am certain love can be broken up into many matters, languages, expressions; and it can be refined to understanding, but when we accept that understanding, the expression is not the goal. We finally allow ourselves to be loved in every sphere of life.

We were created out of love. The fibre of our being is love. But when we are younger or even now, the constant question is: "Who are you to be in love?" and in response we may hear the whisper that the love was never for us. Wrong, broken society. Love is more than deserved or offered, it is more than yours. It is you.

Be careful when things are not done out of love. Love is pure intentions and without ulterior motives. So, when you are ready you will give a pure love, a love untouched by the untrue perspective that love doesn't last or that it is fickle. Don't wonder what it's like to be loved, but start by loving who you are— who you are becoming. Discredit insecurity and make room for more love. Love takes up space, but it is polite, so unless the space is given, it will not dream of conquering.

****

STRUGGLING

Struggling mentally

Struggling emotionally

Struggling eternally

I'm prone to wander and He is prone to chase, but do I wander off a little too far?

Am I less of a human? My thoughts, my heart, my feelings, devastating. Do I accept a free life? Or do I opt for the broken, captive one? Freedom of choice.

Oh, what a Saviour, that would knit and link a story of grace, He would carry me from strength to trial, and carry me effortlessly across the wicked river, my Father a man of great knowledge, too knowledgeable for my understanding. He breaks the shame and slays the giants, God is my faithful Father and protector, from the cradle to the cross, He did it all, He broke the foundation of wickedness and He continued and laid down love, for love is unconditional and cannot be understood, but for love I am grateful. To Jesus be the glory for He is the great I Am and all will know Him.

Position and Disposition

Descriptions:

ALONE — *Having no one else present, on one's own.*

AT HOME — *In one's own home, ready to receive and welcome visitors.*

LONELINESS — *Sadness because one has no friends or company.*

\-

(Of a place) the quality of being unfrequented and remote, isolation.

I have found that being oneself has many benefits, one of which seems necessary and essential when it comes to who you are and identification.

When you know who you are with all rights reserved, the devil has limited resources for temptation. The danger and disposition of loneliness and being alone has a melting edge of sinking purpose when left deserted.

****

1 Corinthians 12:25-27 (NIV)

[...] so that there should be no division in the body, but that it's parts should have equal concern for each other. If one part suffers, every part suffers with it, if one part honoured, every part rejoices with it. Now you are the body of Christ, and each one of you is part of it.

In many ways daily trauma, afflictions, hurt and unnecessary arguments and chatter, can affect the body, intentionally and eternally. I believe that as much as others can hurt us, it's the individual's responsibility in the body to identify, fix and restore the wound. The body can't function properly when one part of it is bedridden and frail. An example of this is forgiveness. Loneliness is a feeling. Feeling alone in a room crowded with people. Being alone is a lie. No one is ever alone. Humans were created for and with community. But God also created His children in His likeness. Meaning a father always stands watch over a child, and even more for a child in need.

Permit, authorise and license yourself to forbid lies of the enemy.

Feelings

- An emotional state or reaction,
- An idea or belief, especially a vague or irrational one.

Often, we act and respond out of feelings, and we are reminded countless times that feelings are a reaction affected directly by an issue or deeply rooted injury that causes the damage of motionless, immobilised, lifeless faith.

AM I

Am I a trophy, a task, a mission or an accomplishment? Is my love not enough, is it unfathomable to recognise its simple nature, to complete professing pure faith which is too rich to contain, too costly to obtain?

Am I too infinite for a limited life, too pure for a fleck of dirt, or am I enough? To carry burdens overbearing, to weigh sin by what I have already paid for? "It's a daily decision child, to choose Me and My yoke. To surrender your life, to restrict the tongue, to be led by Spirit, to be captivated by wonder. To remember who you are."

A culture too cultivated for a love that overcomes the power of strongholds. Neither wickedness nor hell can break love. *"My love is forever"* (Jeremiah 31:3).

Forever:

- For a future, for always, continually (adjective – lasting or permanent)

- "Many forget that My call is not subjective, that a chosen people are being built. Contentment of the world's ways can define your entry, not on My side but on yours. I'm accepting, but when you choose, choose whole-heartedly with a passion ready for a compassionate edge. My people are from all walks of life and when you encounter a fellow brother or sister remember they are already loved and chosen, like you." (No one is excluded from this. However, for further understanding, refer to Ephesians where Paul emphasises pre-destination)

1 John 5:14 This is the confidence we have in approaching God: that if we ask anything according to his will, he hears us. "Before you ask questions, before you seek elite answers. The answers to all questions are to be found by seeking Me. I am the gift and the giver. A journey of life contains the gift and the giver. To unwrap the gift, the gift must be received. So, before you ask questions about My will, ask questions about Me."

****

Hebrews 13:5(b)

"Never will I leave you, never will I forsake you".

A promise is given unto you. A full pursuit of Me is a pursuit worthwhile. In pursuing Me, I pursue you, and when the world stands still and everything and everyone fades; I remain. I am the stability you long for. The wind in the emptiness of night, the passionate fire that makes your eyes fill with tears, and the never-ending love you've been missing. I AM.

I Told God About You

- Crushing/crush
- I think too much
- I feel too deeply

The Difference between liking someone and having a crush on someone?

Liking is more about being attracted to the non-physical attributes of the person (like his or her personality), while having a crush on someone is more being attracted physically to him or her. The feeling of having a crush on someone usually fades away faster than the feeling of liking someone.

Song of Songs 8:4

Daughters of Jerusalem, I charge you: Do not arouse or awaken love until it so desires.

I've had many unspoken thoughts on the idea of having a crush. The bible does not give clear specification on a crush, initial attraction or even on ignoring the feelings completely. My sisterhood speaks openly about who they fancy. I always try to understand whether the feeling is deeper than just physical attraction to physical attributes. If that's the case, then a crush is usually at surface level. However, I have found a particular depth in having a crush.

My Crush

I'd like to think it's more than a crush,

Maybe that's why I tell people to hush,

Simple feelings made complicated by the contemplation of replication.

Could this be true the one I'd like to pursue?

Maybe the attraction was just fascinated but the feelings are not being assassinated,

I'd fall just thinking about you, talking to you,

Whatever shall I do?

Consider this time of reflection, a painting of what could be a true imperfection,

My indecisive mind somehow is sure of this here divisive find.

I have a crush on you,

Maybe I'll tell you,

I have a crush this is true, but surely I can't tell you.

. . . .

A crush makes you shy, a crush makes you giggle, a crush does not change who you are or fiddle,

A crush has uncertain means and for this has space to please,

Anything unnatural could never ease this crushing disease.

Song of Songs 4:16

Awake, north wind, and come, south wind! Blow on my garden, that its fragrance may spread everywhere. Let my beloved come into his garden and taste its choice fruits.

Song of Songs 2:1-2

I am a rose of Sharon, a lily of the valleys. Like a lily among thorns is my darling among the young women.

Joy in Oppression

Psalm 100

Psalm 121

Often being in a single season feels so lonely. The refining of the heart and spirit can feel lighter day by day, but what cures the emptiness of being alone mentally? I feel oppressed, captive to my own motive. How do I become still and enjoy moments with myself? Simple things like a walk, watching the sunset, praying. In these times I choose to never forget what I learnt from the greatly oppressed season of my youth.

A fresh start, a new mercy each morning, the waves haven't swept me away, nor the sea swallowed me, and therefore I have not been broken. I will persist in choosing God. Shake me Jesus, out of my fleshly desire and selfish greed for rushing the streams. Instead restore my weeping so that I may rejoice in being alive. Christ, unless You build my heart, the builders labour in vain. Be not only the Builder, be King, dwell freely in me and work Your biggest, most captivating miracles and good news through me.

2 Timothy 1:7

For God hath not given us the spirit of fear, but of power, and of love, and of a sound mind.

Lord, You continue to speak and minister in lives too arrogant to acknowledge you. But may I never take my eyes off You, for I am Your dwelling place. A fortress for pure righteousness, cords of peace and a slave to holiness. My life is Yours, and I promise to trust Your ways. Master of my every cause, You are my joy. Fill me with joy — not in materialistic achievements but in Your name.

Psalm 131

My heart is not proud, Lord, my eyes are not haughty; I do not concern myself with great matters or things too wonderful for me. But I have calmed and quieted myself, I am like a weaned child with its mother, like a weaned child I am content. Israel put your hope in the Lord both now and forevermore.

VISION

Futures can be daunting,

Either too much or not enough

How do I get where I want to be without coping them or not being too much of me?

Well

To that I'd say

It's who He has created you to be.

And finding vision in the version you are today,

Creates a future for the person you'll be one day.

STAY

Suicide psyche, uncharitable display

Reasoning and judgment pointed a false intimacy toward Yeshua

To conclude, end, resolve or finish predestination, providence and purpose

At the cost of heavens decrease, there shall be none.

To add the value of sheep to the Kingdom of darkness

Suicide subconscious

They not only strip your life but your wonder

Deceitful and untrustworthy are the promises made and burnt up

But true are the promises bound in covenant with El Roi

Suicide perception

Distressed and worried are your burdens

But with hope life invites you

Suicide imagination

Choose truth in its gesture

Don't be persuaded or manipulated into choosing deaths charm

Death tempts and beckons a god of zero

Life exalts the God of all gods.

Suicide ego

Stay a little while longer

Till you've witnessed the wealth of His love

The purity of His heart and the compassion in his eye

Suicidal mind

You are loved beyond measure

Stay

Stay because you can

Stay because it's not the end

Stay because you have hope

Stay because you are not alone

Stay because this is your testimony

Just Stay.

SUICIDE PSYCHE

PSYCHE   The human soul, mind, or spirit.

John 6:64

"Yet there are some of you who do not believe." For Jesus had known from the beginning which of them did not believe and who would betray him.

God is sovereign, and often we are so familiar with His goodness, we do not recognise our flaws. Flaws can reign supreme even though we are handpicked by Jesus, when we have an intimate relationship with Him. In the life of Judas, Jesus was with him in the flesh. We have the privilege of the Holy Spirit, but just imagine seeing with your own eyes, to behold in full the whole world, blink after blink. I recognised that Judas allowed his own holiness to pursue life elsewhere.

Luke 10:18-20

He replied, "I saw Satan fall like lightning from heaven. I have given you authority to trample on snakes and scorpions and to overcome all the power of the enemy; nothing will harm you. However, do not rejoice that the spirits submit to you, but rejoice that your names are written in heaven."

****

SUICIDE SUBCONSCIOUS

SUBCONSCIOUS Of or concerning the part of the mind of which one is not fully aware, but which influences one's actions and feelings.

John 6:70-71

Then Jesus replied, "Have I not chosen you, the Twelve? Yet one of you is a devil!" (He meant Judas, the son of Simon Iscariot, who, though one of the Twelve, was later to betray Him.)

What influenced Judas? He was a man of character and stature to be amongst the twelve. Judas takes away more than he gives. Judas operated out of selfish intent and consumed those around him without convincing them. I didn't know the man, but I know that a man's heart in a moment of weakness is different from a man's heart when he is strong. God had grace for Judas, he was part of the prophesy to betray Jesus, he remains selfish when he still does not recognise the Jesus he has walked with. He chose death, fully knowing life.

****

SUICIDE PERCEPTION

PERCEPTION   *The ability to see, hear, or become aware of something through the senses.*

-

The way in which something is regarded, understood or interpreted.

John 12:6

He (Judas) did not say this because he cared about the poor but because he was a thief; as keeper of the money bag, he used to help himself to what was put into it.

****

Perception is necessary, when you sit near the King, you are His inheritance, you are among His people, and you are subject to inside information. It's important that your perception not be clouded. Things become less clear, gloomy. You start mistaking a gift given to you for safe keeping and nurturing, for a network that will increase your self-control and credibility. You trade a humble declaration for one of unbelievable worth.

Matthew 13:44-45

"The Kingdom of heaven is like treasure hidden in a field. When a man found it, he hid it again, and then in his joy went and sold all he had and brought that field. Again, the Kingdom of heaven is like a merchant looking for fine pearls. When he found one of great value, he went away and sold everything he had and bought it."

****

SUICIDE IMAGINATION

IMAGINATION   The faculty or action of forming new ideas, or images or concepts of external objects not perceived by the senses.

Matthew 26:14-16

Then one of the Twelve— the one called Judas Iscariot— went to the chief priests and asked, "What are you willing to give me if I deliver Him over to you?" So they counted out for him thirty pieces of silver. From then on Judas watched for an opportunity to hand Him over.

Imagination and conflicted thought, reality and action, these components are linked and can wreak havoc. It's unlikely for imagination or an idea to stay in your head once it represents itself in the flesh. Unkindly, the imagination will be guiding your steps, rather than your conscious mind. Years of divine holiness and teaching will now be paid off with just thirty pieces of silver and a betrayal of posture. Life is rhythm, and decisions and actions made to hurt people and even your own interests, can be fatal. Judas plays the role as traitor. His life has not been written off because of what he did, we can learn from Judas, no amount of money is worth your soul, no amount of money or attainment is worth your Saviour. I wish Judas was reminded of the forgiveness that was taught. Judas is no longer, but for us that remain, remember the forgiveness that has been taught.

****

SUICIDE EGO

*EGO   A   person's   sense   of   self-esteem   or
self-importance.*

Matthew 26:47-50 (NIV)

While He was still speaking, Judas, one of the Twelve, arrived. With him was a large crowd armed with swords and clubs, sent from the chief priests and the elders of people. Now the betrayer had arranged a signal with them: "The one I kiss is the man, arrest him." Going at once to Jesus, Judas said, "Greetings, Rabi!" and kissed Him. Jesus replied, "Do what you came for, friend."

Judas used his closeness and association with Jesus as a way to provide for himself. He sacrificed his relationship and allowed it to decompose in utter disrespect towards the man who showed him new mornings. Before Judas saw who he was, Jesus knew and still chose him. Despite who we truly are, God chooses us. Choose Him in return; I don't say that for you to be condemned. I say it for you to reconcile the fact that we can't out do Jesus, His goodness runs deeper than the anatomy of the Earth. We may not understand, but don't make irrational decisions based on a need or want. God has always committed himself to being our Provider in every sphere. The enemy can offer earthly wealth that is depreciated once it leaves his hand. Jesus offers wealth in eternal life that is everlasting, radiant and that fully satisfies.

Luke 15:8—10

(The Parable of the Last Coin) "Or suppose a woman has ten silver coins and loses one. Doesn't she light a lamp, sweep the house and search carefully until she finds it? And when she finds it, she calls her friends and neighbours together and says, 'Rejoice with me, I have found my last coin.' In the same way, I tell you, there is rejoicing in the presence of angles of God over one sinner who repents."

****

SUICIDE MIND

MIND   *The part of a person that enables them to be aware of the world and their experiences, to think and to feel, the faculty of consciousness and thought.*

-

A person's ability to think and reason, the intellect.

Matthew 27:1-10

(Judas Hangs Himself) Early in the morning all the chief priests and the elders of the people made their plans how to have Jesus executed. So they bound him, led him away and handed him over to Pilate the governor.

When Judas, who had betrayed him, saw that Jesus was condemned, he was seized with remorse and returned the thirty pieces of silver to the chief priests and the elders. "I have sinned", he said, "For I have betrayed innocent blood." "What is that to us?" They replied. "That's your responsibility."

So Judas threw the money into the temple and left. Then he went away and hanged himself.

The chief priests picked up the coins and said, "it is against the law to put this into the treasury, since it is blood money." So they decided to use the money to buy the potter's field as a burial place for foreigners. That is why it has been called the Field of Blood to this day. Then what was spoken by Jeremiah the prophet was fulfilled: "They took the thirty pieces of silver, the price set on him by the people of Israel, and they used them to buy the potter's field, as the Lord commanded me."

****

My wishes to be here no longer exist

My heart bears grief, sorrows and troubles unexplainable

My thoughts contain a pain of progressions undesirable

I'm in jail

My flesh is pail

I collect stickers of baggage and place them on the devils reward card

Where I am is light, yet darkness follows me like a shadow

Can anyone else not see a single sparrow?

The rivers of Hope are drying up like a famine stricken plain

I'm in a neighbourhood of dream homes, but my house is burning

On fire

It's my responsibility, I have lit the match.

...

Oh but I love HIM

Surely He opens my eyes and life's persecution feels bearable

He understands

With full knowledge

He is able to lift my head

He is able to carry my heart

He is able to consume my mind

He has made me able.

A suicidal mind confronts or joins the go-ahead decision. Emotional constraint, mentally faint, and physically unaware. A suicidal mind is a desire to live. To live where it is easy, to live where the air is light, to live where the heaviness no longer exists, where there isn't any more life to confront. No more nights of despair, loneliness, where comfort of any sort is not missed.

Mark 15:33

At noon, darkness came over the whole land until three in the afternoon. And at three in the afternoon Jesus cried out in a loud voice, "Eloi, Eloi, lema sabachthani?" (which means: "My God, My God, why have you forsaken me?")

Mark 8:34-38

Then He called the crowd to him along with his disciples and said: "Whoever wants to be my disciple must deny themselves and take up their cross and follow Me. For whoever wants to save their life will lose it, but whoever loses their life for Me and for the gospel will save it. What good is it for someone to gain the whole world, yet forfeit their soul? Or what can anyone give in exchange for their soul?"

Mark 8:31

[…] the Son of man must suffer many things […]

Deep within our hearts we miss understanding the divine. We lack the capacity to control our own unique thoughts. As life and death stand face to face. Remember not just the offering of Jesus Christ but the promise of God to send a saviour. To suffer many things. To suffer all things. Jesus relates to his children with depth, transparency, comprehension and appreciation. He daily walked in flesh with every temptation, flesh, spirit and blood. To not recognise Jesus is to not recognise yourself. We are His kin. Jesus bore our identity whilst walking in his own. Jesus, nature can testify, heavens can confirm and His children are an example of the wonder He is, a gift too good to be true, a gift for everyone, a gift that keeps on giving, and a face we have yet to meet. It's not your responsibility to understand God; it's your responsibility to trust him, to be obedient and to be faithful. Decisions made by God are absolute, he knows everything past, present, future, and beyond, He is infinite and cannot be wrong.

For further study:
Mark 14:10
John 13:18-30
Luke 22:1-6

....

Acts 1:12-26 (Matthias Chosen to Replace Judas)

Then the apostles returned to Jerusalem from the hill called the Mount of olives, a Sabbath day's walk from the city, when they arrived, they went upstairs to the room where they were staying. Those present were Peter, John, James and Andrew, Philip and Thomas, Bartholomew and Matthew, James son of Alpheus and Simon the Zealot, and Judas son of James. They all joined together constantly in prayer, along with the women and Mary the mother of Jesus, and with His brothers.

In those days Peter stood up among the believers (a group numbering about a hundred and twenty) and said, "Brothers and sisters, the Scripture had to be fulfilled in which the Holy Spirit spoke long ago through David concerning Judas, who served as guide for those who arrested Jesus. He was one of our number and shared in our ministry." (With the payment he received for his wickedness, Judas bought a field, there he fell headlong, his body burst open and all his intestines spilled out. Everyone in Jerusalem heard about this, so they called that field in their language Akeldama, that is field of Blood).

"For", said Peter, "it is written in the Book of Psalms:

May his place be deserted, let there be no one to dwell in it, and may another take his place of leadership."

"Therefore, it is necessary to choose one of the men who have been with us the whole time the Lord Jesus was living among us, beginning from John's baptism to the time when Jesus was taken up from us. For one of these must become a witness with us of his resurrection."

"So they nominated two men: Joseph called Barsabbas (also known as Justus) and Matthias. Then they prayed, "Lord, you know everyone's heart. Show us which of these two you have chosen to take over this apostolic ministry, which Judas left to go where he belongs." Then they cast lots and the lot fell to Matthias, so he was added to the eleven apostles."

Mommy

A week of a scar to show me who you are

A bleached body, torment stricken and joy ridden

To bear my praises of a hope unknown

Mommy

With every bit of weight lost, you added love that did not count the cost

Mommy with every meal wasted and just tasted you continued to please my stray appetite

Mommy

You cart parts of me I cannot explain, parts of me that know no pain, parts of me that in my world and heart pertain

Mommy

You sow samples of material I can't conquer and make the word of God clear so that this work shall not devour

Mommy

To you I owe a lifetime of gratitude

Mommy

In a week of weakness, God showed me a lifetime of purpose

Mommy

To you I make this true that my life, I shall live to bid your right-hand adieu.

Isaiah 9:6-7

For to us a child is born, to us a son is given, and the government will be on his shoulders. And he will be called Wonderful Counsellor, Mighty God, Everlasting Father, and Prince of Peace. Of the greatness of His government and peace there will be no end. He will reign on David's throne and over his kingdom, establishing and upholding it with justice and righteousness from that time on and forever. The zeal of the Lord almighty will accomplish this.

SCARED

Scared of what people think

Scared of what people say

Scared of what people do

Scared of what I might not be

Scared of what I fail to see

Scared of a safe living

Scared of a conscious giving

Scared of my only being

Scared of my seed not seeding

Scared of what I may be

Scared of what I may see

Scared to trust anyone

Scared of not being enough

Scared and frightened I may be, but Jesus Thy hand covers me and leads my heart, You sway my liking and love my only capacity.

Scared no more, for scares are the days that lie ahead and much is the labour to be tended

Should I die before my work is done, fear would not have stopped me in my very own magnitude.

Psalm 123

I lift up my eyes to you, to you who sit enthroned in heaven.

As the eyes of slaves look to the hand of their master, as the eyes of a female slave look to the hand of her mistress, so our eyes look to the Lord our God, till he shows us his mercy. Have mercy on us, Lord, have mercy on us, for we have endured no end of contempt we have endured no end of ridicule from the arrogant, of contempt from the proud.

It Ought to Be

My life is not what I thought to see

What I know I should be

What I've been taught to see

Could this be?

What have I brought to be?

I fought to supposition, you agree?

I wrought this tree

Please let me free.

Luke 11:29-32 The sign of Jonah

As the crowds increased, Jesus said, "This is a wicked generation. It asks for a sign, but none will be given it except the sign of Jonah. For as Jonah was a sign to the Ninevites, so also will the Son of Man be to this generation. The Queen of the South will rise at the judgment with the people of this generation and condemn them, for she came from the ends of the earth to listen to Solomon's wisdom, and now something greater than Solomon is here. The men of Nineveh will stand up at the judgment

with this generation and condemn it, for they repented at the preaching of Jonah, and now something greater than Jonah is here."

My Loved One

Bernard Jacob Harley

You take up the biggest frame in my wall

You bear the biggest grief in my heart

Your presence and existence is missed yet still felt in every way

A thank you to you for being the best wisdom in flesh I have ever encountered

You were a gift to my life, a fire to my soul and a fountain of joy to my heart

You taught me to wait for love, you showed me how it's done.

I did not have the confidence to speak at your funeral, and unbearable pain accompanied me in that time, but I'm not scared anymore, I don't feel alone anymore, and I will live out all you spoke over me.

Thank you for being; I honour you

And I love you.

I AM FREE

When I think of Jesus I see myself in a field

I for love have learnt to see Jesus in me

And to see Him through me

This is my heart in words

He is the Christians joy

Fine are the feelings unspoken yet consequent in action

Parallel are the actions with words

I may be frail and fleeting yet pale not the heart of wisdom

God

Words cannot fathom Thy heart

Minds cannot bear Thy greatness

Yet free is the heart that is truly free, and pure is the heart that has been refined

I feel free.

1 John 2:1-2 (NIV)

My dear children, I write this to you so that you will not sin. But if anybody does sin, we have an advocate with the Father — Jesus Christ, the Righteous One. He is the atoning sacrifice for our sins, and not only for ours but also for the sins of the world.

Invitation Only

You have not been cordially invited to this or any occasion

See, you are an outcast and will never be accepted into our home or hearts

If that's the case in mine eye, let the lack of a care facilitate my incapable tone for community.

I will prize tables where fellowship and honesty is performed out of genuine feelings.

And if that takes a while, in the meantime my God and I will enjoy others company as a sacred display that will heal wounds of past and present day.

You have been invited to my table, to my party, to my life. As I invite you to be with me, may the invitation of God be extended to you to be here with thee.

Psalm 128

Blessed are all who fear the Lord, who walk in obedience to him. You will eat the fruit of your labour, blessings and prosperity will be yours. Your wife will be like a fruitful vine within your house, your children will be like olive shoots around your table. Yes, this will be the blessing for the man who fears the Lord. May the Lord bless you from Zion, may you see the prosperity of Jerusalem all the days of your life. May you live to see your children's children — peace be on Israel.

Addiction

I've seen what it can do

I've seen what it can become

Addiction in its beckon is second to none.

I've seen it devour dreams

I've seen it decorate schemes

But in all of this God's light beams

Addiction marks a point of distraction

And conquers distance between you and God, and you and you.

Doesn't make sense — confusion stakes the claim for all these things

I can't help but pray

I can't let you go astray

Addiction will consecrate but God will demonstrate the limits of its infection.

Loss: A Fragment of Life that Cannot Be Gained or Equated to Be Less-than

Fragile the heart that grieves a loved one

Tender the soul

Latched onto the last vision

Spread across the mind a painting

The last painting

It's painful, no injury surpasses the loss

Injuries are merely physical

But to lose, to decrease in presence

That's an injury to the soul, a tear in the heart

Words lack comprehension

My heart dwells on the loss for its not scarce

A pain among others, time heals other pains, but loss
will be dealt with in heaven.

Uncle Glen

Kind in nature

Composed in stature

A soft hearted man

With medical scars to tell war stories

Complaints he had few

With much love he grew

Promises he kept, and with faith he stepped

Failure and defeat the devil could not beat

He was never a burden, but

For certain a signature of fine strength wrapped in compassion

To celebrate his life is no tragedy but a true script

Comfort be not one for this God's son to be a soul of pure peace, we bid farewell and pay our dues

A jazz fanatic with musical taste from the heavens

Carried in the heart of God recalling the suffering he now praises

Pull not a thread of shredded years

But delight in the light of a blissful life lived fully for Christ

No questions now remain, for the man we all proclaim, one day we'll hopefully not refrain from doing the same.

Psalm 116:15 (NIV)

Precious in the sight of the LORD is the death of his saints.

Fear Not the Days that Linger

Fear not the days that linger

For they linger not for long

Fear not the things that trigger

For the triggers make you strong

Unexplainable but true the things He can do

The truth must be known, Christ Jesus not by force be new, but with love renew

Choice is your weapon, the peace we inhabit and the consequences we exhibit

Countless moments we make Him proud and may we fall to our knees and cry to him out loud

His word does not stutter, in our steps we utter.

Temptation has no power may the temple heighten the temperature of countless miracles.

We bind the spirit of almost, we bind the spirit of failure, we replace all these things with the revelation of God and favour.

May riches be your portion and restoration be your story
Nurture endurance and seek wisdom.
Press forward in your youth and touch base in this truth

A frameless mould can be shaped in a moment.

May our lives produce the sweetest fruit, may it bring joy to the heart of God, may it cultivate peace amongst nations and may we walk in purpose, justice, faith, truth and love.

Choice by Day, Choice by Night

As this flower fades, a new one is planted

By choice many lessons we shall learn

And by morning the due will have not been earned but granted

For you I'll carry this burden but by your choice, could you keep your word and be certain

No time can be added or borrowed by your own regime

Keep your pinkie promise and your hands clean.

Allow your choice to have roots and foundation, not consequences and condemnation.

Spare the tears for things uncontrollable and for things where you can have a say, come to me and I will certainly show you the way.

But by choices I have made you free, and for some by choice have sent themselves into captivity.

I the Lord will always be committed to your life, and I will always be the way for those who feel they can't get above (2 Peter 3:9, NIV). The Lord is not slow in keeping his promise, as some understand slowness. Instead he is patient with you, not wanting anyone to perish, but for everyone to come to repentance.

Letters to Heaven

A letter to heaven. Heaven became increasingly intriguing to me in my youth, knowing I have someone to meet once again had kept me wondering about heaven and all its mysteries and unknowns. It is in my youth that I am still captivated by the thought of heaven not being the goal. It's the destination and promised land/home/haven but it's still not the ultimate goal. There is no goal; the purpose is to continually seek Jesus because we never fully find Him until He wants us to.

My brother (Caleb Dreyer) described the Kingdom of God as eternal glory, a place you never want to leave. So, my conclusion is: then can we say that the kingdom of God is Heaven, I find that this society and upcoming generation loves the break down, the understanding and education of topics, however when it comes to facts not in line with their opinion, it is immediately less valued or not necessary.

I refer to a current generation because I am not excluded; God reveals to us many things and often our opinion can override the very message God spoke. Do you often write letters to heaven?

Before you think too deeply about your answer, I'll just add that a prayer is a verbal letter to Heaven, it can be a letter/prayer of thanksgiving, lament, confusion, asking or even silence, and it is received by God and never discredited to the urgency or order of the mail date.

Matthew 6:33 (NIV)

But seek ye first the kingdom of God, and His righteousness, and all these things shall be added unto you.

I struggled to understand this verse, not because it doesn't make sense, but it was always received as a second-hand revelation, I had not heard God's depth of this verse for myself and that's why the weight did not matter much. So, when you seek first God's kingdom, the heavens, his empire and his righteousness, then all these things shall be added unto you. Today we find that for many people the things had been acquired, and seeking God came after, I call that messing with the order of nature whether it be intentional or not.

So, in your letters to heaven remember:

Mark 11:24 (KJV)

Therefore I say unto you. What things so ever ye desire, when ye pray, believe that ye receive them, and ye shall have them.

In a direct question to the heavens:

HEAVEN   *A place regarded in various religions as the abode of God and the angels, and of the good after death, often traditionally depicted as being above the sky.*

HEAVENLY   *Enchanting, divine, ecstatic, paradisiacal, beautiful, angelic, godlike, redeemer, the eternal and the holy.*

In your prayers and letters to heaven, your direct verbal letter, stay a bit longer in the aroma and transit place where the heavens open up to receive your letter. Take that blessing as a glimpse of where you will one day be. It's okay to long for heaven and to long for the days without evil and suffering, but while you are still here, remind yourself you are a soon to be heavenly being, meaning this is not your permanent home, so live a righteous and holy life and honour those who are like you, soon to be like you and even those who have the potential to be like you.

Gather your blessings and count them so that you remain grateful to God for making a heavenly dwelling, where you will one day dwell with him. One of my many letters to heaven included a question of purpose and you are reading the answer. Don't despise your letters, all are valid even the ones not yet written.

Bittersweet Moments

Bittersweet moments

Come near, come by

Bow in the presence of God

Fall from High

Kiss mine forehead for tears I cry

I trust you Jesus, may we never die

Abbreviations for things, they pass me by

Pray for me for I held my own sigh

Life surprises me

I never see it coming

He sees in me, what I don't see and what has yet to be.

Allocate my daily response

Time flares like fire providing warmth and light but can be deadly in its bite.

Bittersweet moments

Come near, come by

Reckless park they set your heart apart.

Plunge thy walk with convicted acts

Place my foot on daring soil

Base my used life on a breath of God

For I live not on bittersweet moments alone

But on the trust I have in God, the unseen.

SECRET HEART

Genesis 12:1-3 The Call of Abram

The Lord had said to Abram, "Go from your country, your people and your father's household to the land I will show you."

"I will make you into a great nation,

And I will bless you,

I will make your name great, and you will be a blessing.

I will bless those who bless you,

And whoever curses you I will curse,

And all people on earth will be blessed through you."

Grasp what you read in a prophetic manner. Don't be hesitant on matters that can preserve our family. Join in a conversation, it is polite to respond when spoken to. With God it can be as simple as having faith in the living and spoken word which He has set forth.

A hidden promise is a protection mechanism that will maintain your need for God. No influence other than God will be allowed to set revival in your heart. Heart to heart. A notion of heavenly desire. To construe the style of blessing the Lord pursues in an individual shall be revealed in one's worship. God has an intriguing nature and because we don't have to fight to be loved. We, in return, feel like we are enough. The insecurity of wanting to be anyone else is combatted by the desire to dwell deeper with God, in the heavenly places. No prayer in vain, no heart in pain, and compassion not confined to pre-evaluated sensible experience.

Father, bless those who don't fathom who you are, open their hearts, allow their eyes to see holy mystery. I pray we listen. I pray we wait; I pray we allow Holy Spirit logic. Patients in a waiting room wait to be consulted by a doctor for opinion or diagnosis… It is in this analogy where repentance is simplified.

Repentance is not only laying down your sin, but it is also allowing the emptiness to be filled. The sin to be medicated and killed off by a dose of antibiotics. And the course is to be fully completed.

Breaking your own heart means to worsen the circumstances with negative falsehood and despair. Breaking your own heart can result in you loosing yourself. The fascinating counter is that losing yourself once in a while can revive forgotten about or seldom utilised characteristics that you can give to God. To have a heart for God and for his matters is to have a sensitive heart, but not a frail one. To filter out the debris. To cater to those who need not only a good meal but a fresh one.

A secret heart is a tender heart. A heart to bestow much life and significance. A secret heart allows God to be the only one to know your endless comparisons in need. A heart that does not echo or embrace envy, gossip or wrongdoing. A heart filled with the hope that more of God shall be the overflow.

The war within is broken in the continuation of faith, any contamination is blinded in the consciousness of victory already achieved.

Incapacitated, incarcerated and intoxicated, not by substance but by constraint. Heavily blemished yet the darkness can blind and burden my sight but can't take it away. By hearing I have heard incomprehensible talent being communicated and made plain for understanding. Scattered words mean nothing. Well analysed, strategised and anointed words can change the course of one's life with immediate effect.

Surrounding yourself with loud words from God's word, the silent whisper in His voice and the warmth of His presence may come like preferred music to your ears and a yearning of your soul.

My soul burns for Jesus

For possible cause

To sing His praise

To embrace His heart

To weep at the world

To carry His heart

To function in limitless rooms

To work in grace

To be heavy with passion

To be pregnant with nations.

Pain and discomfort make the victory taste sweeter

The night will not bind your soul

The night will crown your head with dreams and visions unlike mortal comprehension.

The love of God goes far beyond mystery.

The indiscernible King with uncounted, unmatched talents, beauty, knowledge and attributes we have no words to compare. He awakens you in the morning to embark and labour. Don't forget your building gear.

Prescribe scripture as if you were a pharmacist to your physical, spiritual and emotional pains.

Burst with passion and excitement for the oxygen is on its way. Prepare your best and get ready to meet the King. The presence of royalty does not come cheap.

Life by Choice

CHOICE BY DEFINITION   *An act of selecting or making a decision when faced with two or more possibilities.*

Proverbs 3:5-8

Trust in the Lord with all your heart and lean not on your own understanding, in all your ways submit to him, and he will make your paths straight. Do not be wise in your own eyes, fear the Lord and shun evil. This will bring health to your body and nourishment to your bones.

Proverbs 11:1-2

The Lord detests dishonest scales, but accurate weights find favour with him. When pride comes, then comes disgrace, but with humility comes wisdom.

Life by Choice is like day and night

Compatible in the most conflicting way

Peculiar to the most perishable intelligence

In evidence I find verification and submit to the proposition specified

Choice by divine definition and clear detail narrate the degree of importance. Choice.

It so closely depicts freedom from captivity.

Capability from inability/incompetence and

Availability from being laboured or strained.

Choice shapes the means in which He will direct your life.

The strategy in which how much time is set apart for humbling, learning and capacity

Time for struggle and unfiltered weakness.

Life by choice entails freedom and consequence.

CONSEQUENCE BY DEFINITION   *A result or effect, typically one that is unwelcome or unpleasant.*

For further reading: Genesis 3:16-19 (NIV)

Mustard Seed

Matthew 13:31-32

He told them another parable: "The kingdom of heaven is like a mustard seed, which a man took and planted in his field. Though it is the smallest of all seeds, yet when it grows, it is the largest of garden plants and becomes a tree, so that the birds came and perch in its branches."

Matthew 15:21-28

Leaving that place, Jesus withdrew to the region of Tyre and Sidon. A Canaanite woman from that vicinity came to him, crying out, "Lord, Son of David, have mercy on me! My daughter is demon- possessed and suffering terribly." Jesus did not answer a word. So his disciples come to him and urged him, "send her away, for she keeps crying out after us." He answered, "I was sent only to the lost sheep of Israel".

The woman came and knelt before him. "Lord, help me!" she said. He replied, "it is not right to take the children's bread and toss it to the dogs." "Yes, it is, Lord," she said, "Even the dogs eat the crumbs that fall from their master's table." Then Jesus said to her, "Woman, you have great faith! Your request is granted." And her daughter was healed at that moment.

Matthew 17:20-21

He replied, "Because you have so little faith. Truly I tell you, if you have faith as small as a mustard seed, you can say to this mountain. 'Move from here to there', and it will move. Nothing will be impossible for you."

A year of Magic and favour

The fear of losing what you remembered. How can I be happy without Gods will – Bishop T.D. Jakes.

A year of magic can't be fulfilled without faith. The bible describes having faith as small as a mustard seed, I often feel I have greater faith than the mercy filled mustard seed, and yet nothing. God revealed in my heart that it is not great faith that I have built up, but instead expectation and anticipation which is not faith, faith is complete trust in him, an ongoing understanding that God will complete everything according to His will, crafting guidance and a sense of stability in uncertainty.

We are cleansed by the Blood of the Lamb, unified in dignity and clothed with His spirit. The devil is so manipulative, and with his resources he chooses to blind people to destiny and purpose, but remember even the devil forgets he is part of God's MASTER PLAN. We are slaves to time and so is the devil, he does not dwell, he intrudes, he is not intriguing, he is an imposter of perfection. How do you tell?

Use your REAL LOVE to discern, I believe in a humanity that will one day have full and real love for one another, a captivated nature and spiritual outlook on all matters, not just clean, easy or uncomplicated ones.

Plant the kingdom of Heaven in your heart so that it may grow to be the largest in the garden. And when you pour out your heart the heavens align with another soul so that it is to be restored and welcomed back home. Don't put your faith in holy and righteous people of Christ, draw strength and trust from Him first hand, battles are never easy, but they are always won with Jesus. Find comfort in adjusting, in preparing and allow your germinated seeds to be watered and nurtured by God. When God is happy with your faith-seed – your request will be granted. Don't count any day loss but as faith-built testimony. TRUST GOD

Allow your faith to lead you, to lead your life, a God life is filled with faith and trust, meaning little or no control of the individual, sacrifice and surrender, easily mentioned, but troubled hearts struggle to detach love for control and possibility. A downplay on probability, a 50/50 gamble, but with God we are secure.

Empty but not forgotten, faith filled chairs believing in a regroup of unbounded blessing. An outpouring from heaven for those who endured and continue to endure great suffering, continue to sing his praise loudly for relief lingers no more , feel change at the breaking of morning , at the dusk of dawn and at the annual offering of thanks giving, He loves you, He loves us , we are His, He never left, He never will and He is always GOD, shout, scream, dance for joy, for He is our saviour who saved us, and HE will continue to awaken our souls for His good and for the good of those around us. Stay faithful in faithless encounters, Christ is the Lord and He will be praised forevermore, He is the start and finish, the beginning and the end, the potter of the clay, I love you JESUS, you are my faithful friend and Father, anoint me as I fall to my knees, may I have a fraction of the faith You carried as a man on earth to TRUST, may I trust You Jesus, wholeheartedly with outrageous and relentless love for others. AMEN.

Avoid or a Void

God's anointed can't be held back forever.

The Gift of Goodbye – Sarah Jakes Roberts

Job (read whole book of Job for full context and understanding)

Job 1:6-12

One day the angels came to present themselves before the Lord, and Satan, also came with them. The Lord said to Satan, "Where have you come from?" Satan answered the Lord, "From roaming throughout the earth, going back and forth on it." Then the Lord said to Satan, "Have you considered my servant Job? There is no one on earth like him, he is blameless and up right, a man who fears God shuns evil." "Does Job fear God for nothing?" Satan replied "Have you not put a hedge around him and his household and everything he has? You have blessed the work of his hands, so that his flocks and herds are spread throughout the land. But now stretch out your hand and strike everything

he has, and he will surely curse you to your face." The Lord said to Satan, "Very well, then, everything he has is in your power, but on the man himself do not lay a finger." Then Satan went out from the presence of the Lord.

AVOID   Keep away from or stop one from doing (something), repudiate, nullify, or render void (a decree or contract).

VOID   Not valid or legally binding, completely empty.

Everything gone

It's been done

Dust

Nothing but dust

My hopeless state of being

Too weak to cry

Too numb to grieve

Tough times never last, but my tough times seem to have shown up at every waking breathe. Could my love for God cost this much? Choose right. Dead are my hopes and faith. Laying waste while my youth is in the present. I lie barren with nothing to birth, just lost dreams, sleepless nights and constant troubles knocking on my heart, head and unconscious body that also seems to be unconsciously biased, only allowing deep rooted hurt and the trauma of a succession of generations. I long to write love songs, poems and stories. Instead, I lament about things. I don't understand. Stuck in strange places, unknown environments, unfamiliar exits. It's as if I'm meant to find no end; like it's almost perfect placement. Could this possibly be love? Back into your arms again I'll run. In this undisclosed, unrevealed and unspecified location. I will wait. I wait on You God. For I am hidden treasure. Hidden to those who see me. Presented by my Father (God) and resented by Satan.

No End

Lord, I know that people's lives are not their own, it is not for them to direct their steps. Discipline me, Lord, but only in due measure — not in your anger, or you will reduce me to nothing. Pour out your wrath on the nations that do not acknowledge you, on the peoples who do not call on your name. For they have devoured Jacob; they have devoured him completely and destroyed his homeland.

Are not the stars days numbered? Does not anger turn away? For wickedness the clock ticks. For sin the veil tore. Carry thy burden and birth a worry. To Jesus thy burden is given not even a name. Count not the days lost by foul faint fear. Gain to the man who trusts the Lord's eye. For the guiding hand makes for remarkable delight. Does not the star come to an end? Does their light shine for but a season? Capture my wonder Jesus for wonder and mystery can be found in all things You've said, done and to come. Continue thy mind onto the path of recovery. Evil may manipulate and destroy but your Lord is Master. Master of all trades and matters. Conquer fruitful spirits so that one may be a fruitful spirit. In love, truth and purpose continue with Jesus. For His days are not numbered, nor does He come to an end.

Stuck in a Time Zone

Guaranteed a destination. Stationary on a timeline. Like an unsupported promise on a road of clear vision and gold purpose. If you won't ask the question I will. Why am I stuck? My declaration and testimony of life has been about the struggle. Should I struggle any further? Does Thy hand stretch far and wide even for a political, complicated, meaningful daughter? This has become so much deeper than loneliness. Singleness has uprooted death sentences. The enemy has used every weapon, threat and encounter to erase and delete me out of God's will. However, the word of God, even just by memory has kept Him close. All I have needed Thy hand had provided. You always provide.

Direct my thoughts and mind father so that Your inheritance may counter every obstacle, so that Your knowledge can fathom my unfathomable influence that seems unnatural. Take full control of my thoughts.

Help conquer my mind so that my mind does not conquer me. Thoughts linger and pain haunts. The past comes back in my sleep, and the future visits in my visions. Make my mind sober Jesus; strong and on guard for any and every threat. Even when I'm stuck in spirit, truth, wonder and in every faculty. God stands up righteous and ever ready to catch me when I fall. They tear me down, they crush my spirit, they consume my thoughts, but my trust remains in You. I believe that You are building me and renewing the battle that belongs to You. Victory is ours.

Even time will run out on itself, but our journey will continue forever. Your power in my weakness, that makes the darkness tremble, the shadows shine and God is revealed in all who have ever encountered you. By dream, person, angle, Holy Spirit or by song.

Oh, hear my voice God. It may not be soft or full of intellectual complaints, but it is pure in intention and genuine in tone. Be kind when I utter split confusing messages, for my heart has been broken too many times. You are not my last resort; You are my only one. I don't miss days I didn't understand. I feel closer now that I hear you clearly. Continue Your footsteps in my life. You make my path bearable. You are my heartbeat, my love song, and my life. My love for You Jesus has never, and will never be enough, but it's all I have. Receive me gently for I suffer for you. Listen. Listen to the texture of my voice. Time, time fades and my feet started adapting, not being in control. Thank you for choosing me to love you willingly and for listening to my cries. You are my calm, my safe space,

my Holy and abundant beloved. I was born/made/
created to love and serve You and there's nothing I
long to do more.

The Lovers Dream

Lamentations 1:1-2

How deserted lies the city once so full of people! How like a widow is she, who once was great among the nations! She who was queen among the provinces has now become a slave.

Bitterly she weeps at night, tears are on her cheeks. Among all her lovers there is no one to comfort her. All her friends have betrayed her, they have become her enemies.

Lamentations 3:21-33

Yet this I call to mind and therefore I have hope: Because of the Lord's great love we are not consumed, for his compassions never fail. They are new every morning, great is your faithfulness. I say to myself, "The Lord is my portion; therefore, I will wait for Him". The Lord is good to those whose hope is in Him, to the one who seeks Him; it is good to wait quietly for the salvation of the Lord. It is good for a man to bear the yoke while he

is young. [... ...] 30 Let him offer his cheek, to one who would strike him, and let him be filled with disgrace. For no one is cast off by the Lord forever. Though He brings grief, He will show compassion, so great is his unfailing love. For he does not willingly bring affliction or grief to anyone.

Offer the desires of your heart to God as burnt offerings. Sacrificing distraction and selfishness to complete your own will. Cast out every plan of new levels of life and success and replace them with reflection. Erase those ugly knots in your heart, that create rites of passage to destruction. You are capable and willing. This is the lover's dream that you utter not just words of love but actions of truth.

Doubt not the lover's dream, for it was built on trust. That He would create you and me in His perfect image and position of gifts, that He would set you free and allow you to choose Him or not. A God that when confusion came, he met you halfway. Suffer your way to success and satisfaction. Making God proud is not winning a Nobel peace prize, nor is it even completely considering the poor and weak. Proud is God when you choose to carry His will with jubilation. God will show you the way. Proud is God when you trust in him. My late grandfather always said 'every house has it's cross' and I believe so does each individual, not just in Christ. Proud is God when you don't carry it alone. When accepting His helping hand. Don't cast yourself down because of the Lover's dream. Be confident in it.

I thought the concept of a lover's dream was the idea I had of love, a specific person, way or language. I was wrong. The lover's dream is the word with both action and truth. With added stories and most beautiful revelation of who God is. The Lover's dream quenches a thirst, divides hunger, and creates everlasting intimacy where expression is encouraged, so that others may find themselves in you and therefore be drawn to your source. This is the Lover's Dream that you love and dream.

LOST FOR WORDS

Philippians 2:6-11

Who, being in very nature God, did not consider equality with God something to be used to his own advantage; rather, he made himself nothing by taking the very nature of a servant, being made in human likeness. And being found in appearance as a man, he humbled himself by becoming obedient to death — even death on a cross! Therefore, God exalted him to the highest place and gave him the name that is above every name that at the name of Jesus every knee should bow, in heaven and on earth and under the earth and every tongue acknowledge that Jesus Christ is Lord, to the glory of God the Father.

Resign myself to it. Contain my frame to it. Made on incredible work to establish and pursue the message of God. Show up for Jesus.

Silent whisper Thy comfort. Contain not Thy warmth. Chains are cast down, for this anointing has reached preparation peak. Counter Thy enemy, wicked thought stealing vision. Awaken my spirit. Bring my visions to life. When did You know the world needed one of me? My mind has not reached full consciousness yet. I don't know who I am. But I have a clue in the bubble of self-gain and increase. Credit and glory to EL Roi, Jesus, the name above every other name. Amen.

All praises to the Lord of open doors, a dimension of myself I have never seen in my life. However, I step into my position comfortably with ease and peace, as if I was the missing puzzle piece that fits right in. An unrecognisable piece of art now brought to life and affirmed with the blessing and favour of God, changing the world and its patterns since the day she was born. He was with me all along.

Hear my victory devil. I am anointed to bring hope and good news for the captives that have been bonded and manipulated. How selfish and how like the devil, to blind mankind from their Creator and God even though you have to give account to the I Am.

Your days are limited (devil), your days are numbered. You try and try to knock me out, but this freedom was fully paid for. So, stop stealing mankind's salvation. The God of Israel is near, and he carries victory like an undefeated stallion. King of the waters, nations and everything under, over, in and above the sun. Unseen and unknown He is King and He will reign forever. Listen devil for your God still speaks. Lost for words devil? Out of tricks and schemes?

You are not one to give up. Your pursuit of my life and cause aligns with what God had spoken over me in my youth. You see devil I realised who I am. Singleness, loneliness, anxiety, depression, temptation, trauma, pride and grief only brought me closer to my Lord. So listen devil for your God still speaks.

Stumbling into Your New Role

STUMBLING   *Tripping or losing balance while walking, moving with difficulty.*

NEW   *Produced, introduced, or discovered recently or now for the first time, not existing before.*

(Read 1 Samuel 17 for full context)

1 Samuel 17:33

Saul replied, "You are not able to go out against this Philistine and fight him, you are only a young man, and he has been a warrior from his youth."

Ever felt out of place? An outcast figuring out identity and life, in this true story David is unannounced and anointed and his position in the spirit has not come to pass naturally; David, pure in heart and wise in mind is always misunderstood and deliberately made out to be evil with poor intentions.

1 Samuel 17:28

When Eliab, David's oldest brother, heard him speaking with the men, he burned with anger at him and asked, "Why have you come down here? And with whom did you leave those few sheep in the wilderness? I know how conceited you are and how wicked your heart is, you came down only to watch the battle."

David was consistent in faith and in his belief in God, he did not question God in the mundane days, he knew that God doesn't waist an anointing.

Psalm 12:6 (KJV)

For every word God speaks is sure and every promise pure. His truth is tested, found to be flawless, and ever faithful. It's as pure as silver refined seven times in crucible of clay.

It's this assured heart that carried purpose into presence. I believe one's status or position in life or sphere, can bring insecurity when challenged, thus blinding the spirit and not allowing for clear and assured discernment. It's in this insecurity that we find many people stagnate. People start replacing the idea of faith and full trust in God with favouritism and comparison, in this we not only question if what God has given us is good enough but we question if it's better than the old-timer, we also question God about whether He favours one of His children above the others. One would think we need not question our Father on His interests, He has taught grace and therefore whatever has tenderised our hearts, he comforts us with understanding.

Favouritism: The practice of giving preferential treatment to one group at the expense of another, the state or condition of being the competitor thought most likely to win a sporting contest.

Favouritism can be a heart ache or niggle in one's heart for a season or even many seasons. With favouritism comes the idea or concept of only one of the best, planting a seed of doubt and a decreased confidence.

Romans 2:11 For God does not show favouritism.

Just because God doesn't show favouritism doesn't mean people won't, we are mere human beings and can unintentionally show a certain liking or love for a particular person over another. I challenge your mind with this thought. Though they favour me not, may peace attend my way, whatever God has placed has every right to be favoured. **God gives each of His children equal gifts and is counting on you and me to use our gifts to be a blessing and win souls for Him.**

Though misunderstanding latched my hearts anchor. I now fully recognise that it is not for man to favour me or my gifts, but those rights are reserved for the one that has given them (the one and only true God)

So, even though the favour of mere mortals is not to your advantage — it didn't help David. I'd rather be an outcast than be far from my purpose. You are anointed and not yet announced but as you walk your purpose into the present remember who anointed you and who favours you. He is the one who knew the world would need you and that not only a task, but a life's mission of ministry needed your assistance and initiative. Don't be downcast at a lack of support.

STUMBLING   Moving with difficulty.

1 Corinthians 10:13

No temptation has overtaken you except what is common to mankind. And God is faithful; he will not let you be tempted beyond what you can bear. But when you are tempted, he will also provide a way out so that you can endure it.

Modesty and the Art of Expression

A LIFELONG VALLEY

Have you ever felt as if you've been more in the valley than on the mountain top? While circumstances cling to you like a newborn baby to its mother. Consistency of a particular process becomes draining and when seasons feel similar you stop learning, and therefore stop leaning on God. You gain the independence you were never meant to have and become confident in an imaginary fixation on a thing or things that won't last.

MODESTY   *The quality or state of being unassuming in the estimation of one's abilities.*

-

The quality of being relatively moderate, limited, or small in amount, rate or level.

-

Behaviour, manner, or appearance intended to avoid impropriety or indecency.

ART   *The expression or application of human creative skill and imagination, typically in a visual form such as painting or sculpture, producing works to be appreciated primarily for their beauty or emotional power.*

-

The various branches of creative activity, such as painting, music, literature, and dance.

EXPRESSION   *The action of making known one's thoughts or feelings.*

I need you to pay attention!

The treasure of the ages. How do we recover the things we have lost? How do we retrieve the treasure beneath the sand? Can art be modest? Can one fully express oneself with limitation? The most powerful weapon is the weapon of identity. I believe this to be true. Besides appearance humans express their differences through character. The Spirit will operate in your lack or weakness. So no, art cannot be modest, nor can expression be limited. As a Christian young woman, I have had to navigate modesty, boundaries and resilience.

We are called to represent Christ. I struggled with the suggestion, which then implies the objective or recommendation that we should all be identical or alike (culturally and systematically). The manner or approach I consider, is that we are called to represent Christ but at the same time not disregarding our own unique character. I believe art can be true to the artist. Art illustrates the artist. What he was thinking when creating, how he was feeling unfolds in the articulation and statement. Mouthing utterance of inner detail. How God wanted his children to represent him. Hair, style, speech, conduct and individuality.

What you are passionate about and how you carry yourself may not lead millions of souls to Christ, but it will influence the souls around you, so that people who don't necessarily fit in also have someone to follow, and lead them on the right path of life, so when it comes down to modesty in this modern world, allow your art to blossom through expression with a God confidence. Reach, Teach and Preach. Stand tall with your creations for you are the heir of the best, most well-known, world renowned and appreciated Artist in the universe.

I HAVE

Have you ever watched their admiration for Him

Their longing and love for Him

Their pleading

Their praise

Their worship?

Have you ever watched the causes being brought before His judgement?

The countless thanks being professed

The blessings of knowing and loving Him

The answers being given

The faith being filled

And the pain seeping from their flesh?

Have you ever seen Him move like that?

I have

Has He ever promised and delivered?

Has He ever taken away and not given better?

Has He ever made you dream and have it come quicker; helped you pursue?

I have.

Hebrews 6:13-20

The Certainty of God's Promise

It Wasn't Supposed to Be Me

I shouldn't have fallen for you

I did everything there was to do

To block all these feelings from you

But it's me that couldn't see

You were all I ever needed to be free.

To fall in love

Gosh it rests like a dove

On shoulders this heavy

My palms are so sweaty

Now, how do I explain?

I can be a pain and also very vain

Definitely not a plain Jane but you get this chain

Starting to sound like a train
What I am trying to say is

It wasn't supposed to be me
I mean however could it possibly be?
We were only ever going to pass by
Until you never said
Goodbye.

I am in Love with You

I am in love with you
But every moment we've ever had
I've left feeling blue
You haven't given me a reason to love you
But I do

I love all your faults
They are what make you
You

They've hurt me though
And even though I don't want to
I must go

To be loved in return
That's when love truly burns

You could do anything but also nothing
And I'd melt
But everything I've ever felt

Has made me cry for help
Because of you

This can't be love
When it's not felt in return

It's made me realise
This is what the Father feels as well
Through His kindness thick and swell
The love never draws back from many
But He continues to tarry

So shall I
Sorry we didn't work out together
And I'd never say never

But between you and me
This has been too hard
We're not meant to be but
GOD HAS US
Together or Never

Loving you I'll never grow tired of
However
I am going to find someone
That loves me better.

Be Seen

I see you

Your beauty surpasses your pain

But I see you

I hear you

Your knowledge surpasses your understanding, but I hear you.

Don't let deaf ears disperse your words

Don't let blind eyes over-look your confidence and bravery

I see you

I hear you

More accounted for, more accurately and more accessible

God sees you, your audience of one, God hears you, your esteemed guest of one.

No inaccurate information cow your imagination, for he sees the imaginable and infatuated wonder of your life.

Obedience

I considered obedience to be the bricks of submission, surrender and meekness. The foundation of obedience is agreement.

AGREEMENT

1. Harmony or accordance in opinion or feeling.

2. A negotiated and typically legally binding arrangement between partied as to a course of action.

3. The absence of incompatibility between two things, consistency.

CONFIDENCE

1. The feeling or belief that one can have faith in or rely on someone or something.

2. The telling of private matters or secrets with mutual trust.

OBEDIENCE

Compliance with an order, request, or law of submission to another's authority.

Ezekiel 12:21- 28

There will be No Delay

The word of the Lord came to me: "Son of man, what is this proverb you have in the land of Israel: 'The days go by and every vision comes to nothing?' Say to them, 'this is what the Sovereign Lord says: I am going to put an end to this proverb, and they will no longer quote it in Israel.' Say to them, 'The days are near when every vision will be fulfilled. For there will be no more false visions or flattering divinations among the people of Israel. But I the Lord will speak what I will, and it shall be fulfilled without delay. For in your days, you rebellious people, I will fulfil whatever I say, declares the sovereign Lord.'"

The word of the Lord came to me: "Son of man, the Israelites are saying, 'The vision he sees is for many years from now, and he prophesies about the distant future.' Therefore say to them, 'this is what the sovereign Lord says: None of my words will be delayed any longer, whatever I say will be fulfilled, declares the sovereign Lord.'"

The negligence and rebellion against God's will and purpose is disobedience. The longer we delay God's work, the longer we deprive God's people of hope and salvation. The rhythm of a life is obedience. Obedience is discipleship when one is quieted and settled to get it right. Not just for the benefit of God and His plan but for the benefit of those He dearly loves, which therefore includes an abundance of souls untouched and untended by our gentlemen Holy Spirit. He touches and commits a level of trust and expectation to the finer details of an individual's life where sin and wickedness is not considered. This takes into consideration the lives overtaken by weaponries, demons and demon like spirits that carry a mandate of influence where safety and security in Jesus can be seen, found and accessible. Learn the art of service where obedience is a consistent agreement with God, saying yes to Jesus, until you breathe your last breath of mortality. Don't break your life's rhythm for temporary people and gratification. There will be reminders in one's life that echo God's promises in fulfilment.

I recognise that in a life of obedience shame is recessed, and success in spiritual warfare is undeniable. Your light heart will abide in obedience and will therefore thrive in abundance.

Obedience ordains peace and compassion for even the most judgemental, in our obedience and agreement God opens our eyes to things we have never seen before. It's more than a change in perspective, it's something we've missed along the way, to be subconsciously arrogant is a gamble, when one is not aware of costly actions that can set us back, we may find ourselves disconnected from God and in those moments we cannot pinpoint where we got stuck. We, as the body of Christ, have been called upon to complete our assignments, if we knew what these assignments are, we would fit ourselves into boxes of perception, making the outcome unnatural, we ordain it and the glory would be for ourselves, how challenging for natives to consume or receive from a foreign giver with no knowledge of the culture, language or tradition. It's in the processes where we relearn and unlearn, where God can lead and guide, so that the voice comes from the native him or herself, from the inside, where people are more open to listen and accept. Trust the process and lean toward obedience, allow God to bring intellectual understanding and patience, where strategy in knowledge is obtainable and is steered by the spirit. Your emotional reality is not your future state of abortion; don't allow frustration to collapse your substructure.

Ephesians 1:11-12

In him we were also chosen, having been predestined according to the plan of him who works out everything in conformity with the purpose of his will, in order that we, who were the first to put our hope in Christ, might be for the praise of his glory.

Seek Him obediently, with discipline and wonder.

RENEWAL THEOLOGY (book) — J. Rodman Williams (Ref.)

Since the background of all theological reflection is the living God in relationship to the living creature, theology seeks to unfold Christian doctrine as a living reality. It is not, therefore, the architecture of inanimate mortar and stones nor the structure of a beautiful but lifeless cathedral, it is rather the articulation of living truth in all of its marvellous variety and unity.

God, is ultimately beyond our comprehension; thus, there will inevitably be some element of mystery, or transcendence, that cannot be reduced to human understanding.

Theology is an intellectual discipline, and thus involves reflecting upon and ordering of a certain area of knowledge. It is one way of loving God with all of one's mind (Matt 22:37) and thus a mental labour of love that seeks to set forth, as coherently as possible, the ways of God with man. Theology, accordingly, is "Faith seeking understanding".

Nothing else is required, just full faith, trust and obedience.

HELLO

My name is Jemma

And on most days, I particularly enjoy the weather

Whether it be shine or dim

I don't mind, as long as life's chances don't grow slim.

I've always had a strong sense of who I am and I'm now old enough to know

That opportunity won't just come because it can

Instead we are shaped as if we were moulded in a master's hand

A constant becoming

If life were up to me, it would've ended a long time ago

Not because I didn't enjoy it

But because I wouldn't know where to go

Where do I go from here?

An answer only He would know

Well He was an ancient story once told

That took place maybe 2000 years ago

UNTIL

He opened up my eyes and truth breathed on me

HELLO

HISTORY

I've been a history fanatic since I could remember

It's why Law has been an ember

I love it because it's what has happened

And it calls us to be better

It shows visions of war, victory, oppression, peacemakers and days that have ended.

History has left room for people to be offended, amended, and has allowed Glory to be descended.

I look back at the past and just know that from beginning to end

Through faith, failure, fashion and famine

It's HIS-story

That's why I love it.

Admiration for the Wounded

Inspired by the clouded heart.

People never really get to know you, do they?

Really know you

Really walk with you

Really talk with you

Not quite like Jesus can

People never really get to know you, do they?

The real you, the raw you, the core you

The more you

People never really get to know you, do they?

The pure you, the flawed you, the cold you

People never really understand you, do they?

When I say God has been good to me, good is the understatement of the century

Good cannot begin to explain how devoted God is to me

How much I feel his demonstrated love

He is superior to any satisfactory and excellent feeling of love, hope, care and valid meaningful influential opponent which he has also created for his Glory.

Are the prophesies being fulfilled

Are those in question answering with death?

Don't fear, for the written word describes your victory in great detail

A clear and painted framed picture of your end

Unity is near

Love will prevail.

People may never understand your depth and intention, the Creator of your very nature uses your clueless frustration to save those who suffer from blindness, remember what He said — King Jesus remains.

Psalm 121:7

The Lord will keep you from all harm.

I Scream Jesus

I scream Jesus

I scream my Lord

Don't harm my heart

Don't plough that which has been cultivated in and by perfection

Why do you misinterpret the prophesy

Why does realisation come too late

I scream Jesus

My hopes and dreams

My unfiltered wind of bliss and unconditional love

My fragrance and light

My morning Song

That the day would have passed

When on a hill my heart would carry my world

How heavy the cost

How painful the disrespect

I scream Jesus

You move my heart

You light up my life

You increased my service

You please my every desire

I scream Jesus

You chose me

You love me

By humble mind and heavenly scribe

God has ordained thy walk for a long while

For a period

Find Him — Those who search for Me will surely find Me. (Proverbs 8:17)

Love Him

My Jesus

My Lord

How He was so much more than I ever imagined or even dared to imagine

My heart was harmed and persecuted for those that idolise dust and sand

Break their heart to open up your life to discover, feel, and realise the depth of my Jesus.

1 Peter 3:12

For the eyes of the Lord are on the righteous and his ears are attentive to their prayer, [...]

Love is "Sacred"

Sacred describes something that is dedicated or set apart for the service or worship of a deity, considered worthy of spiritual respect or devotion, or inspires awe or reverence among believers. The property is often ascribed to objects (a sacred artifact that is venerated and blessed), or places (sacred ground).

I have found that sacred, can also be remembrance of past events or historical occurrences; so when I refer to the sacredness of Love, I am referring to Jesus on the cross, but also to the very beginning; creation and the love and intimacy God is, but Adam was.

An author with a true idea and capacity but lacks the ability to articulate, has no story. People respect you on the level of your articulation. Love is received on the level of your sanctification. In the book of Leviticus, we are reminded of the importance of detail in honouring. Clean and pure offering and sacrifice. God has created life full of detail. Though the detail may not assure your knowledge of order and patience.

It shows the detail of renewal God creates in us day by day. I believe God defies law and natural order. Priceless, timeless and righteousness. Things an eagle of nations will not condemn. For power does not lie in a clouded and faint mind. But in a mind open to seeking and discovering the treasure at the end (not always hidden, plain site can be blinding)

Our reward is not just riches, it's everything your and my heart desires, it is everything your imagination imagines. And it is satisfaction paid in full.

Psalm 45:1

My heart is stirred by a noble theme as I recite my verses for the King, my tongue is the pen of a skilful writer.

Leviticus 6:9

The Lord said to Moses: "Give Aaron and his sons this command: these are the regulations for the burnt offering: The burnt offering is to remain on the altar hearth throughout the night, till morning, and the fire must be kept burning on the altar."

Regardless of comfort, the instruction is to KEEP THE OFFERING ON THE ALTER AND THAT THE FIRE MUST BE KEPT BURNING.

How many convictions and simple instruction, directing the life of the world should we need more of.

Independent of comfort, should the enemy attack the very sanctification we need, how much damage and corruption are we actually in. Unclean inside and out. We go from birth and innocence, to growing up and being hurt(damaged), and then trying to regain that purity.

Life is in dire need of this very CLEAN LOVE, not just untainted and perfect, but a love that is offered and can heal wounds, cancel ill concentration and erase those very impurities we continue to reproduce.

Consider the name, consider the thought, consider the punctuality, consider the endurance.

A moment where God shall comfort thy weeping and you shall be the vessel that conquers the very thing that crippled and paralysed your spirit. Cruise through the waves of worry and doubt. The ocean is filled with more than roaring waves and high, high waters.

Fill your heart with the words of your Father, so that your heart may overflow with divine motivation, allow yourself to live a life free of anxiety. Express yourself and tell your story. For it is not lack of expression that crippled and halted your story. It was the power struggle. The internalised venture of "WHO I AM".

I have realised it does not matter WHO I AM, as long as I find myself in the "I AM" I will always know the who.

****

Isaiah 40:3-5

A voice of one calling: "In the wilderness prepare the way for the Lord; make straight in the desert a highway for our God. Every valley shall be raised up, every mountain and hill made low, the rough ground shall become level, the rugged places a plain. And the glory of the Lord will be revealed. And all people will see it together. For the mouth of the Lord has spoken."

Isaiah 40:11-14

He tends his flock like a shepherd: He gathers the lambs in his arms and carries them close to his heart, he gently leads those that have young.

Who has measured the waters in the hollow of his hand, or with the breadth of his hand marked off the heavens? Who has held the dust of the earth in a basket, or weighed the mountains on the scales and the hills in a balance? Who can fathom the spirit of the Lord, or instruct the Lord as his counsellor? Whom did the Lord consult to enlighten him, and who taught him the right way?

Who was it that taught him knowledge, or showed him the path of understanding?

Remember Your Name

How pure the heart of an innocent mind. How accomplished the mind of a seated peace. Sonic the time flies, rich in reality, the possessions of fruit. A constant urge to do more. To be more.

To advance and increase. Decipher the paper for a pen. Create the drop rather than the drip.

Dribble the courage to drizzle the flow. Draft the template for creation. The microphone can't produce without the wisdom. The penny can't drop without the incline.

Falling: An act not many are fond of. What if it's in this fall we orchestrate and adapt to what it's like?

A method between mathematical conclusions. Identify the feeling and position your focus. For a stage needs its manager. Unsettled direction can only lead nowhere.

Where's the script? The rewrite? Do I play my part? Or do I rob my associate's end?

Do I abandon my calling and try to play the character I didn't even audition for. Is this role play too much. Too real, too raw.

Can one fade this far away? My mind so constantly consumed by everyone's end, that I cannot even see my next step, let alone picture the finish line or frame my after.

I long for the days of Justice, truth and fairness. For the days where love is the deepest of depth.

Why does the sensation of emotion isolate a response. I don't think that fear is in failure. I think that fear comes from threat. A hostile infliction to recite words of worry. When I remember my name

Jemma, Dove

The dove represents peace of the deepest kind. It soothes and quiets our worried or troubled thoughts, enabling us to find renewal in the silence of mind.

My name is Jemma. What's yours?

Faith in Quietness and Full submission

1 Timothy 2:11

A woman should learn in quietness and full submission.

QUIETNESS — *- Absence of noise or bustle, calm.*

- The fact or state of abstaining from speech.

FULL SUBMISSION — *- An act of submitting something (as for consideration or inspection).*

- The condition of being submissive, humble, or compliant.

- An act of submitting to the authority or control of another.

God often has His people in positions of wonder, where we are enhanced to shine. Quiet wisdom selects the heart that is willing. Where emptiness is the only offering. The breath of heaviness carries a summons of barrenness cultivating the source of all laceration. Reasons for instruction will disqualify the season. I have always wrestled with the notion of being quiet and submitting fully to philosophy that does not make mention of my narrative. I felt it was appropriate to vilify consumers of raw told falsehood and deception. I took on the responsibility of protecting my own heart from injustices not even advocates can justify in a court of law. I bled an encore of victimisation. Beyond my jurisdiction I amend my attitudes to find true depth in the core (nucleus) of which my animation is built. The source of all wellsprings. I despise wrong doers and hosts of devilish acts, who carry particles of evil. I have learnt and accepted that my flesh is weak, but my spirit was made to see God's glory in all resolution. Trees created to grow and germinate, uplifting the very existence of ALL life on land. The inhalation and exhalation experienced in our lungs can be held hostage if the very purpose of trees and plants of the same pursuit were challenged. My stubborn downfall of characteristics, being bothered by everything that brings discomfort. Growth is tampered with and damaged if discredit is open to perform.

1 Timothy 2:15

But women will be saved through childbearing — if they continue in faith, love and holiness with propriety.

In moments of great despair, I have added that whispers of heaven are not often heard, but they are always felt. To be clouded in mystery, and drowning in unpatched wounds, with worries bigger than mountains, can have names of former fears and failure. A familiar and natural purpose and position cripples the hearts of many women when childbearing is forbidden or withheld. A common occurrence and outpouring of figuring out how to do the very thing described to be your purpose. From what I have known to be true growing up, the biggest blessing to barren women is a child of her own by blood. I think this ideology has greater depth. A philosopher will increase their knowledge on an incomplete idea to add critical, analytical and argumentative skills to an already complex hypothesis. To me the most tortuous escapade is when the soul is withheld or forbidden its most organic and innate desire to birth an idea, design, dreams, undiscovered articulations, ambitions, stories, testimonies and prayers. I trust that God's will is unwavering and conveys every transaction to a sustainable end.

1 Timothy 4:4-5

For everything God created is good, and nothing is to be rejected if it is received with thanksgiving, because it is consecrated by the word of God and prayer.

It is sometimes difficult to alter the mind into accepting the view that nothing is rejected if it is received with thanksgiving. If positive notions and theories are the outlook of this very statement, racism and social issues that criticise, manipulate, attack and dehumanise people's identity, will be abolished. I reconcile my own embedded tales of colonisers and lay to rest the idea that it would ever happen again. People being oppressed because of differences in skin pigment and being treated differently because they are helpless and therefore not being helpful to the next person but adding a burden of needs that can reach different extremes. Laws have been made and past to transform and create a new justice system where we are all seen equal in the eyes of Law, but some people just can't see past what someone else is or lacks. I have, in moments in my life, seen and experienced this weight that paralyses mortal personage and I have great compassion for them. It is destructive to hate certain distinctive traits in another human and can also create anxiety. I think we as humans have made a mockery of the simple task of just loving people for who they are and who God created them to be, and the damage is deeper than that. A place and seat in heaven won't cost your soul another soul. Damage control starts in the heart of the oppressor and the oppressed. After forgiveness, thankful and grateful hearts will knit the body and army of God together and will gather and provide for those who find themselves in a constant state of confusion and distress. Not just an asylum but a home of constant consolation. May we see the good God created, with peace, love, kindness and respect.

1 Timothy 4:12-16

Don't let anyone look down on you because you are young, but set an example for the believers in speech, in conduct, in love, in faith and in purity. Until I come, devote yourself to the public reading of Scripture, to preaching and to teaching. Do not neglect your gift, which was given you through prophecy when the body of elders laid their hands on you.

Be diligent in these matters; give yourself wholly to them, so that everyone may see your progress. Watch your life and doctrine closely. Persevere in them, because if you do, you will save both yourself and your hearers.

Hearers   Those who hear what someone else says.

The embrace of your Father is like no other, the solace in his presence will shift your stance to an upright posture, a space where you separate your trial from your name. To see the affair from an outside viewpoint and to allow God to use your story. Be consistent in the way you work, love, speak and the way you appear. I know it's good for the heart to have a healthy soul to count on when the heart is being refined. Devote yourself to the Lord's proceedings, you are part of the body and contribute by just existing and taking up space. We may experience the powerless feeling when evil overtakes the affair of the season. Council your heart for hard and challenging times that will arise. But don't lose hope, for joy comes in the morning and those who sow in tears will reap in joy. In a single season, good separation of matters will correct the selfish feeling pressurising you to be more than you are in this current space. I believe God prepares our hearts, minds and overall wellbeing to elevate His glory.

This book has referred to love in an overwhelming manner to demand its understanding. We were created in love; we are to die in love, and I believe we are here to represent love. In an official capacity to plunge darkness at the root, to defuse hate, to disrupt the emptiness, and for people to look back on love and realise that salvation is not enough, it's not the end, salvation is the beginning of our stories, we found in Jesus. When we attain the knowledge of who He is, He will come again. In the meantime be obedient, trust him, love him, and worship him in your greatest dimension. Build, declutter and honour.

Titus 3:1-11

Remind the people to be subject to rulers and authorities, to be obedient, to be ready to do whatever is good, to slander no one, to be peaceable and considerate, and always to be gentle toward everyone. At one time we too were foolish, disobedient, deceived and enslaved by all kinds of passions and pleasures. We lived in malice and envy, being hated and hating one another. But when the kindness and love of God our Savior appeared, He saved us, not because of righteous

things we have done, but because of his mercy. He saved us through the washing of rebirth and renewal by the Holy Spirit, whom he poured out on us generously through Jesus Christ our Savior, so that, having been justified by his grace, we might become heirs having the hope of eternal life. This is a trustworthy saying. And I want you to stress these things, so that those who have trusted in God may be careful to devote themselves to doing what is good. These things are excellent and profitable for everyone. But avoid foolish controversies and genealogies and arguments and quarrels about the law, because these are unprofitable and useless. Warn a divisive person once, and then warn them a second time. After that, have nothing to do with them. You may be sure that such people are warped and sinful: they are self-condemned.

My Single Seed

In the words of Paul in 1 Corinthians 7:31 – "For this world in its present form is passing away."

In Conclusion, I've had many conversations with fellow believers on the notion of "THE ONE" and in all honesty I have excluded the knowledge of Google when it came to this tale. I think the imagination of an individual can add many scenarios to this tale to limit reality of our own personal conviction. I believe that I am praying for a specific person when I pray for my future husband, and I believe I am praying for the specific children in my future care whether it be by birth or adoption. Therefore, I do believe in the one, not as one specific person, that narrows God's will, but with faith that God will protect and nurture my future while I continue to become independent, established and to walk in full purpose without controlling or worrying about that aspect of my life. It is completely possible for people to wander from God's will, and choices have a massive impact not just in our day-to-day life, but in our future and the roles we will play, what features and details of our life will be personified. Therefore, it is of the utmost importance that you pray over your future and to have sympathy on bad choices you have made so that you can learn and grow from those precious assignments. God's promise will still be fulfilled in your life.

1 Corinthians 7:8

Now to the unmarried and the widows I say: stay unmarried as I do.

Paul's urgency for an extended single life made me realise that expression of declaration and conformity saves the heart and mind from premature corruption. An extended single seed will allow you to invest increasingly and fruitfully into yourself, becoming pure with a clean heart, creating healthy boundaries, and extinguishing commitment, trust and loyalty issues, developing patience, relating to past traumas and finalising contribution and service to God. Start speaking life and abundance into your world (Proverbs 18:21 "The tongue has the power of life and death, and those who love it will eat its fruit"). Create a philosophy of signal fire praises to God, making every moment in life one of opportunity to thank God for new and old mercies, for present and past graces and for the overflowing love that became tangible to human kind on the day He gave his life for us to be saved, renewed and free. No one left behind, no one left for dead.

1 Corinthians 7:17

Nevertheless, each person should live as a believer in whatever situation the Lord has assigned to them, just as God has called them.

Conflict at heart can steer the mind in many different directions. Often we find ourselves in downward spirals, replaying moments in our lives that we view as failure, where we beat ourselves up for not being where we want to be, or obtaining a certain status. What if we write a final chapter of control and lay to rest the fraction of our lives that we thought we fully knew. I think God is so mysterious and wildly vast, He can take the most involuntary trampling of mourning and make it joy; He counts our ocean by the amount of waves, not by the pollution we did not welcome or create, he flushes out all the disaster after great endurance. One thing I remember about my grandfather is his sloppy wet kisses; I would not tolerate that type from anyone but him. In the same way tolerate God's passion, for it means well, a plan with God will never end. A lifetime of endurance can generate strain, but it can also fabricate character. Character development and preparation of the Lord's proceedings will outlast even the devil's most particular assignment. Live freely in full belief that Jesus Christ is the saviour of the world even if persecution settles, our people in the bible withstood persecution and so can we.

1 Corinthians 7:23

You were bought at a price, do not become slaves of human beings.

The individual self is categorised as a human being, so don't become a slave to you. We are God's dwelling place when we offer God the leeway. When welcoming a guest into what is already theirs, the only protocol is to greet, provide hospitality and accept. I have many times been misunderstood by people, not because I wasn't being myself, not because I'm different, not because I'm unwilling to open up to people, but because of the other persons disregard for interaction; in life we will not get along with everyone, but if we have a common interest that is the centre of both lives, a line can be drawn and met at. Don't become a slave to people, their opinion of you, their disregard or disrespect for you. You know who you are, and you carry yourself in the grace that was afforded to you by Jesus Christ. Don't allow offence to consume your heart, people are forgiven. Be moved by what God has placed on you during council and be diligent in doing these things with a clear mind, heart and with passion.

Proverbs 18:22

He who finds a wife, finds what is good and receives favour from the Lord.

I am reminded that I am meant to change and evolve, to expand in seasons, collecting all my lessons, celebrating my small victories and that barely recognising who I am, at times is necessary. I now know who I am in every aspect, I know what I want, I know not to entertain and mislead people I know God did not plant in my future.

In this single season it wasn't about finding someone, it was about finding you, truly knowing who you are, who you can be and loving every aspect of yourself, good or bad. The essence of being princesses in this palace is that you understand and discern your role and its reason. Spiritual achievement is not often supported by competition of an opposite likeness. The impressive distress women can go through and still come out wearing their crown, counts victory in its own right. As a woman of colour I have noted that representation is principal. Representation is acceptance. Refusing to embrace representation is refusing diversity. When representation is not visible people can struggle to relate to condition or common duty and may not see their obstacle in others. Representation can have many faces and aura, not just skin colour; people were made not to be the same, but that doesn't mean our differences have to separate or segregate us. Find representation in the inclusion of hope. You represent generations to come.

To my person, I'm still waiting for you, and I will continue to wait, until our destiny and purposes cross. The prayer of my heart for you is that you find Jesus in the deepest of depth, that you pursue your dreams, and that you don't struggle with blessings that are rightfully yours.

5 different crowns that are earned by handling life God's way:

The imperishable crown – 1 Cor 9:25

The crown of Exaltation – 1 Thess 2:9

The crown of Righteousness — 2 Tim 4:8

The crown of Life — James 1:12

The Crown of glory — 1 Peter 5:4

Let me and my life be a testimony of a single season that can truly impact your life. A dyslexic child who struggled with the task of reading and writing. Only God would use a little girl like that to write a book to guide others the same way God has guided her. I've endured indescribable pain and I found myself cautious of creating because of this. But God's will is unwavering, and no fleshly or demonic being can stop his plan for your life

Written with and in love.

Jeremiah 29:11

New International Version

11 "For I know the plans I have for you," declares the Lord, "plans to prosper you and not to harm you, plans to give you hope and a future."

The Prayer of My Heart for You

Dear young women (because we never really get old.)

Go after the passions that allow all your senses to be alert. The passions that allow other people and God to shine through you. Be picky with what you allow in; only give space to sparks that will light up your soul and life. Be careful of damaging sparks that burn the things you treasure most.

Life is not a game. Playing with life can be fatal to your purpose and can crush your spirit.

Grow in God's work and theology. Create a prayer life that will build your character and the strengthen your faith. Be obedient and carry your integrity with full confidence in Christ. You can do absolutely anything. Grow into being and toward the women you have always wanted to be, but never neglect who you are.

God is the steel structure and pillars that keep the house up, but He is also the solid foundation. God doesn't look down on you so don't look down on yourself.

Friends don't always stay, and friends can change your life; be wise.

Focus on the people that are in your life right now rather than the people who are not. Remove the pressure to be perfect and just be you. Grow in compassion and admiration; don't grow tired of loving people. Show up and be kind.

A message I would tell my younger self:

Be yourself and allow yourself to be.

Dream even bigger.

It's not your fault.

Don't be arrogant but rather be considerate.

Gentleness is not weakness.

You may not understand now, but God perceives you as he created you.

In Awe

In awe I am

In awe I stand

Psalm 91:1

Whoever dwells in the shelter of the Most High will rest in the shadow of the Almighty.

Words On a Page

Words on a page
It's all I have for you.
Nothing but words on a page
It's all I could do.
Words on a page to show you
He can do it for you too.

2 Samuel 23:1-7 (NIV)

THE LAST WORDS OF DAVID

These are the last words of David: the oracle of David son of Jesse, the oracle of the man exalted by the Most High. The man anointed by the God of Jacob, Israel's singer of songs. "The spirit of the Lord spoke through me; his word was on my tongue. The God of Israel spoke, the Rock of Israel said to me: 'when one rules over men in righteousness, when he rules in the fear of God, he is like the light of morning at sunrise on a cloudless morning, like the brightness after rain that brings the grass from the earth.'"

"Is not my house right with God? Has he not made with me an everlasting covenant, arranged and secured in every part? Will he not bring to fruition my salvation and grant me my every desire? But evil men are all to be cast aside like thorns, which are not gathered with the hand. Whoever touches thorns uses a tool of iron or the shaft of a spear, they are burned up where they lie."

Life May Come
Life May Go

Life may come life may go. Troubles may come troubles may go. The power of the tongue is what I know. Courageous storms they pass me by, but in Him I know to fly. Try my Jesus try my Lord. For His curtain can't be torn. Faith filled daughter I'll carry you home. Look up at me I calm the storm.

Count thy blessings for they come not cheap. Step into the water for it goes deep. Character, character I say:

Charge thy sin into the nearest hay/chamber

Walk in love , walk in life

For Jesus is still thy tribe.

If I Could, I Would

If I could change places with you I would

To replace you and release you from the pain of this burning wood

If I could reach out and show you just how much I care

I would run miles in the rain and maybe even shave my hair

If I could purse your heart as if it were mine to begin with

I could create stories of where to meet you

If I could change the world to show you I loved you

I would

If I could do it for you once and for all so that you would never have to

If I could be the one you come see every time you go astray

I would do it over and over and over again

Just so that sin would never feel the same

The reality of it is

He can and He did

And declared that it is finished.

Authors Bio

Jemma Dreyer is a 22-year-old law student from Cape Town, South Africa, who never thought it possible to write a book. Her passions include all things Jesus, justice and theology. Her dream is to be an advocate for those who cannot help themselves, and through this hope, to generate a bigger and greater love for Jesus in the world. Through this book, she wishes to inspire women to navigate single seasons and guide them to find wholeness and healing.

This book is an act of obedience. The author therefore does not claim to have experience in writing or literature. The significance of this book serves as a journal allowing females to process their single seasons, leave the past behind, grieve loss, find forgiveness, and recognise the blessing of this time. To find themselves established with joy, lessons, happiness and above all – God. Manifesting whole women through Christ, ready to take on the world in every domain under every earthly and heavenly sky.